D0488539

# Action For Care

## A REVIEW OF
## GOOD NEIGHBOUR SCHEMES IN ENGLAND

# Action For Care

## A REVIEW OF GOOD NEIGHBOUR SCHEMES IN ENGLAND

### Philip Abrams, Sheila Abrams, Robin Humphrey, Ray Snaith

THE VOLUNTEER CENTRE

First published in 1981 by
The Volunteer Centre
29 Lower King's Road,
Berkhamsted, Herts HP4 2AB
England

This book is copyright under the Berne Convention. All rights are reserved. Apart from any fair dealing for the purpose of private study, research, criticism or review, as permitted under the Copyright Act, 1956, no part of this publication may be reproduced, stored in a retrieval system, or transmitted, in any form or by any means, electronic, electrical, chemical, mechanical, optical, photocopy recording or otherwise, without the prior permission of the copyright owner. Enquiries should be addressed to the Publishers.

Copyright © Philip Abrams, Sheila Abrams, Robin Humphrey, Ray Snaith 1981

ISBN 0 904647 14 5

Typeset by Cylinder Typesetting Ltd, London.
Printed in Great Britain by Cylinder Press, London

# Acknowledgements

Many people have helped in the compilation of this report. First and foremost, we thank the organisers and secretaries of Good Neighbour Schemes up and down the country who have patiently responded to our requests for information. Janice Davinson and Fred Robinson, both former members of the Rowntree Research Unit at Durham, played an active part in the early stages of the study. Craig Whitehead, formerly of the University of Durham Computer Unit, provided essential assistance in the analysis of our data. As usual, we are deeply indebted to the Joseph Rowntree Memorial Trust for the basic support it provides for the Unit. This particular survey was funded by the Department of Health and Social Security as part of a larger study of Patterns of Neighbourhood Care. We are grateful to Giles Darvill, Sara Gurrey and Ruth Hunter for advice. Paula Lewthwaite of the Department of Sociology and Social Policy at Durham provided secretarial assistance beyond the call of duty.

# Contents

# I
# Introduction

Trying to describe Good Neighbour Schemes is rather like trying to write a report about Unidentified Flying Objects. Many people claim to have seen them, but there is no general agreement about what they are – or, indeed, whether they really exist. So we should begin by stating as clearly as possible what *we* mean by a Good Neighbour Scheme. So far as this report is concerned, a Good Neighbour Scheme is *any organised attempt to mobilise local residents to increase the amount or range of help and care they give to one another.* Such attempts can take many different forms and can be sponsored and organised in many different ways. In fact, one of the questions that crop up again and again when Good Neighbour Schemes are discussed is whether any one form of organisation is more likely than others to achieve the common objective. To define Good Neighbour Schemes in terms of their aims, as we do here, rather than in terms of their specific activities or administrative arrangements, allows one to begin to answer such questions, by comparing the different ways in which various groups have pursued the shared purpose.

Good Neighbour Schemes, as so defined, are part of a larger, wide-ranging movement to promote "neighbourhood care" that has built up since 1970. In fact, efforts to promote neighbourhood care had been made much earlier than that: the "Good Companions" of the WRVS, the "Link" schemes of Age Concern, and the many projects sponsored by various churches, voluntary bodies and community groups, would all have their place in a comprehensive history of the subject. In a sense, "Good Neighbour Scheme" is no more than the currently fashionable name for a type of venture that has been around for a very long time. In another sense, however, the degree of public interest in neighbourhood care, and the consequent degree of commitment to organised Good Neighbouring, that has developed since 1970 is indeed new. This recent phase perhaps begins with the Report of the Seebohm Committee (the Committee on Local Authority and Allied Personal Social Services), which called, in unprece-dented and unequivocal terms, for "a community-based and family-oriented service" that would "enable the greatest possible number of individuals to act reciprocally, giving and receiving service for the well-being of the whole community". More specifically, this pioneering Report stressed both "the importance of community involvement" and "the need to encourage in-formal 'good neighbourliness'" as essential features of the new pattern of social welfare that it envisaged. Since the publication of the Seebohm Report in 1968, that theme of encouraging good neighbourliness, of drawing an ever-wider range of local residents into an ever-wider variety of caring and helping activities, has acquired a dramatic new emphasis in almost all areas of social policy. It has been taken up vigorously by many voluntary and statutory organisations. The Volunteer Centre – itself a product of the 'post-Seebohm' spirit in social policy – has made neighbourhood care the focus of a three-year programme of work. And, most spectacularly, the Secretary of State for Social Services, David Ennals, announced in the autumn of 1976 the launching of a national "Be a Good Neighbour" campaign. The campaign seems to have been far more than just a routine ministerial gesture; it received strong personal support from Mr Ennals, and secured quite remarkable publicity and backing. This report will *not* attempt to assess, or even describe, the results of David Ennals' campaign. Nevertheless, the way in which he launched and promoted it did much to define Good Neighbouring in its 'modern' sense. Beyond the welter of badges, posters, handbills and leaflets, beyond the exhortations to individuals to "pluck up your courage and be a good neighbour", beyond the national advisory group of leading voluntary and statutory bodies that backed the campaign, beyond the Campaign Unit set up in London to co-ordinate activities and keep up the flow of advice, information and publicity, one fundamental aspect of the exercise was its direct encouragement to local residents to form organisations in order to promote mutual help and care, and its equally direct encouragement to Social Services Departments and voluntary organisations to support such efforts. In other words, the "Be a Good Neighbour" campaign firmly established Good Neighbour Schemes on the agenda of social action. Within the larger movement to cultivate neighbourhood care, it gave an explicit role to grass-roots helping and caring, to direct action by local residents within their localities. It demonstrated ways in which Seebohm's notion of "community involvement" in neighbourhood care could be more than just a pious hope.

That demonstration was important, since "neighbourhood care" can have meanings that are quite unconnected with the notion of neighbourly action by neighbourhood residents. It can, for example, mean bringing about closer contact between social workers and their clients by re-organising social work on a "patch" basis; and to some politicians, it can mean a cheap alternative to professional or residential care. By contrast, the aspect of neighbourhood care that is emphasised in Good Neighbour Schemes is not so much that of delivering services more efficiently or more cheaply, but quite simply that of *a more neighbourly society,* a society in which the locality is the setting for help and care by and among local residents. It is, in fact, a direct attempt to "enable the greatest possible number of individuals to act reciprocally for the well-being of the whole community".

This attempt is not necessarily at odds either with the aim of providing a more comprehensive and efficient delivery of social services, or of reducing the cost of the welfare state, but is certainly different from either. By defining Good Neighbour Schemes in terms of local neighbourly action we have chosen to emphasize that difference. Our justification for doing so is the survey described in the following chapters: this revealed that, in recent years, within and around the framework of established statutory and voluntary organisations, a new initiative has taken shape – a drive towards the renewal of neighbourliness. Good Neighbour Schemes are in the vanguard of that initiative.

Since there is no fixed definition of a Good Neighbour Scheme, we had to begin our attempt to map the national distribution of Schemes in an exploratory way. Allowing ourselves a year and a strictly limited budget, we set out to find as many Good Neighbour Schemes as we could. Our first problem was where to turn for information. Although the publications of The Volunteer Centre and the "Be a Good Neighbour" campaign gave the impression that there was a huge and rapidly-increasingly number of Schemes, neither the Centre nor the Campaign Unit had anything like a comprehensive listing. And although in some areas Community Associations, Social Services Departments or Councils of Voluntary Service had compiled detailed guides to neighbourhood care in their districts that allowed us to estimate reliably the numbers of projects meeting our definition, we found that no such guides existed for the great majority of areas. So we began by writing to the obvious statutory and voluntary sources, restricting our attention to England. We contacted all the Departments of Social Services, all the Councils of Voluntary Service and Rural Community Councils, the area offices of the National Federation of Community Associations and all the Volunteer Bureaux, asking them for information about neighbourhood care projects in their areas, and specifically for the addresses of the organisers or secretaries of such projects. This exercise produced a list of just over 3000 neighbourhood care projects that seemed, from the rough-and-ready information supplied, to fit our definition of Good Neighbour Schemes. We then sent questionnaires to the organisers of all these projects, asking about their aims, activities, organisation, funding, composition and problems. By the end of this second exercise, we possessed fairly detailed information about 1026 groups or organisations which, we felt, could be described as "organised attempts to mobilise local residents to increase the amount or range of help and care they give to one another". This report discusses those 1026 Schemes. They are, of course, only a fraction of the total number of Schemes in existence. Although the response to our first round of enquiries was very good (about 80 per cent), the information given was often patchy; and in the second stage, the response rate was only 58 per cent. So we have done no more than skim the readily-visible surface of Good Neighbour Schemes. Can those 1026

Schemes be considered as representative? We think that they can, for a variety of reasons. The gaps in our information are not concentrated in any particular region, nor are they associated with any specific statutory or voluntary source that has initiated Good Neighbour Schemes or with which the Schemes normally co-operate. After our first round of enquiries, Berkshire, Birmingham and Northumberland remained conspicuously blank on our map; it is difficult to see why. The gaps revealed in the second stage were no less random. At neither stage did it seem necessary to infer that the Good Neighbour Schemes we did not know about were significantly different from those we knew. But it must be admitted that, quite apart from the problem of non-respondents, our map gives only the main contours of Good Neighbouring. This is partly because our questionnaire sought only basic information about the Schemes, and partly because the Schemes reported to us were patently only a fraction of those operating in the areas concerned. In a few cases – either because a Scheme sounded particularly interesting, or because we were convinced that the information supplied did not give the complete picture for a locality – we followed up our postal enquiries by visits to specific towns or counties. These visits invariably demonstrated that many more Schemes existed than had been brought to light by our letters and questionnaires. In one city, for example, from which we had received information about only one Scheme, our visit revealed to us the existence of a further twenty-six! But to have covered the whole country in this way would have been quite beyond our resources. So the information presented here must be regarded as the visible tip of the iceberg. To the best of our knowledge, however, it does cover the general outlines of the subject. Alongside our map of the overall incidence and distribution of Schemes, we have included brief case studies of several Schemes, in order to bring out some of the detail that might otherwise have been lost.

The report has five main sections. Chapter Two presents the general findings of our national survey of Good Neighbour Schemes, concentrating on their origins, organisational characteristics, functions, funding, size and distribution. Chapter Three draws on the more "qualitative" findings of the survey to explore the problems common to Good Neighbour Schemes and to consider the conditions that enable Schemes to realise their aims successfully. Chapter Four comprises six short case studies of Schemes that seem particularly representative of the major types of project, or that reveal with particular clarity the special problems that face all Good Neighbour Schemes. Chapter Five brings together statements by several national statutory and voluntary agencies about their policies towards neighbourhood care in general and Good Neighbour Schemes in particular. And finally, in Chapter Six we present our conclusions and speculate about the future.

For those interested in the details of individual Schemes throughout the country, we have prepared, as a companion volume to *Action for Care*, a *Handbook of Good Neighbour Schemes in England* (also published by The Volunteer Centre) that briefly describes almost 200 Schemes and gives the names and addresses of useful contacts. We did not attempt in this handbook to provide a *comprehensive* listing of Schemes, for various reasons. Firstly, of course, we were well aware that the Schemes we know about represent only a fraction of the national total. Secondly, many Schemes have a relatively short life-span, and even those that survive for years can change character quite dramatically in the course of time. And, finally, some of our respondents were clearly unhappy about details of their Scheme being included in a published directory. So our *Handbook* describes simply a selection of Schemes – although they are of all types and from all parts of England. Furthermore, only Schemes that we ourselves consider to have been largely successful are included.

# II
# A Thousand Good Neighbour Schemes

Our first discovery from the survey was that Good Neighbour Schemes are committed to a distinctive common purpose that marks them off from other types of local voluntary organisation. Like those organisations, they seek to improve social care within their locality by using local residents to provide help and support. But, *in addition*, they seem to share the hope that, beyond any particular services which they provide, one result of their activities will be *a general increase in neighbourliness*. They draw on local residents not only to offer specific forms of help to one another, but also actively to promote general "neighbourliness". This ideal does not depend upon participants being neighbours in the strict sense; few schemes insist on help being given by or to people who are literally next-door neighbours. Rather, the idea is to encourage "neighbourly acts" within the locality; the unit of neighbourliness is not households next door to each other, but the street, the estate, the block or the village. That is the level at which the majority of Schemes seem to envisage a renewal of the spirit of neighbourliness. Hence, we are dealing with a type of social care project that is distinguished from others not only by its use of local residents to provide help for other local residents (the basic definition we adopted in our enquiries), but also by its use of that provision of care as a means to the more general end of cultivating neighbourliness. That was one of the most striking findings of our survey.

Between January 1979 and March 1980 we received information about 1026 projects that we felt fitted our working definition of Good Neighbour Schemes. Unfortunately, as already mentioned, the information was supplied in a variety of ways, and not all of it was suitable for formal analysis. In what follows, therefore, the quantitative evidence refers to only 830 Schemes, while the more qualitative evidence draws on all 1026; such are the demands, and limits, of statistics!

This chapter is divided into three sections: (i) a general outline of the characteristics and functions of Good Neighbour Schemes; (ii) a consideration of how Schemes originate, and how they are affected by their various origins – in particular, by their involvement with the statutory social services in their locality; and (iii) an examination of the distribution of different types of Good Neighbour Schemes throughout the country.

Before going any further, we should perhaps mention nomenclature. Good Neighbour Schemes are, in fact, given a wide variety of different

14

names by their members and organisers. The majority have, admittedly, settled for the obvious "Good Neighbour Scheme" or "Neighbourhood Care Group". But a significant minority have been more inventive. Some Schemes have incorporated their main service function into their name; for example, "The Nursery Workshop", "The Home From Hospital Scheme", "The Housebound Club", and "Concern For The Elderly". Others have emphasised their locality and their objective of neighbourliness; for example, CONTACT ("Call On Neighbours To Assist and Care Today"), "People Next Door", "Friends and Neighbours Scheme", "Neighbourhood Group" and "Village Care". Some church Schemes have adopted names with a religious connotation: "Towards Fellowship", "Christian Contacts in the Community", "Social Responsibility Group" and "Serving and Caring". The importance of reciprocity in Good Neighbour Schemes was emphasised in such titles as "Jobswap" and "Give and Take". Perhaps the two most creative names we encountered were "Homebasket" and "The Availables". The mere names of Schemes are perhaps a trivial matter; but many of them do serve to reinforce the themes of locality, service, reciprocity and informality that are the special characteristic of Good Neighbouring.

## The General Characteristics and Functions of Good Neighbour Schemes

Among the first questions we asked was "When was the Scheme set up?". We assumed that the majority would have been founded as a result of the dramatic growth in publicity and advocacy for Good Neighbouring during the years following 1976. But the survey proved us wrong, as Table 1 clearly shows. In fact, 421 Schemes (50.8 per cent of the 830 Schemes for which we have quantitative data) were set up before 1975 and, of them, 69 were founded more than 20 years ago. Since 1975, moreover, Schemes have been launched at a steady annual rate: between the beginning of 1975 and the end of 1977 262 Schemes (31.5 per cent) were set up (an average of 87 per year) and in 1978 86 (10.5 per cent) Schemes were founded. Although only 41 (5 per cent) of our 830 Schemes were set up in 1979, this does not necessarily imply a slowing-down; our information-gathering was spread over the whole of that year, so presumably more Schemes were being set up after the relevant agencies in their area had replied to our inquiries.

*Table 1*

*When was the Scheme set up?*

| | | |
|---|---|---|
| Within the last year (1979) | 41 | (5%) |
| 1 – 2 years ago | 86 | (10%) |
| 2 – 5 years ago | 262 | (31%) |
| Over 5 years | 421 | (51%) |

15

Generally speaking, it seems that neighbourhood care, in the form of Good Neighbour Schemes under whatever name, was already well-established before the campaign of 1976 and that, since then, there has not been the growth in numbers of Schemes that was presumably hoped for.

Our second set of questions concerned the functions of Schemes and the type of people helped. We asked in quite general terms about each of these topics, thus giving respondents considerable flexibility in how they answered. Had we been more specific, we might have received, for example, a more comprehensive list of tasks and client groups; but specific questions tend to prompt the answers that researchers expect, so, on balance, we felt that general questions would evoke the most meaningful replies.

*The vast majority of Schemes were engaged in home-visiting,* which they saw as a primary activity; 632 respondents (76 per cent) listed it as one of their principal functions and, indeed, 39 (5 per cent) said that visiting was their *only* function. The concept of a "neighbourly" project seems particularly closely associated with the practice of "popping in" to other people's homes. Visits may be either occasional, to solve a particular problem, or regular, to visit someone who is lonely, housebound or isolated. However, the hope of most Good Neighbour Schemes seems to be that occasional visits will develop into a long-term relationship as deeper needs and common interests are discovered; this development is widely regarded as a criterion of a successful Scheme. And, if visiting is the core activity of Good Neighbour Schemes, *the elderly are clearly their core client group;* 681 informants (82 per cent) mentioned that they helped the elderly and, of these, 552 (66 per cent) listed visiting among their principal functions. But visiting the elderly is by no means the whole story. Most of our respondents reported a wide diversity both of functions and of types of client; indeed, only three respondents said that they did nothing else but visit the elderly. Visiting is not so much an end in itself for Good Neighbour Schemes as a way of opening doors both to "neighbourliness" and to the provision of other specific services.

Of the latter, *transport* is by far the most widespread; 374 Schemes (45 per cent) said that they provide transport and, for seven Schemes, it is their only function. Many organisers seemed surprised at the importance transport assumes in their Scheme's work. But there is a substantial gap in the welfare state's provision in this respect – a gap that Good Neighbour Schemes seem particularly well-suited to fill. It is a question of connecting people in need with the services designed to care for them: the hospitals, clinics, doctors' and dentists' surgeries, opticians' consulting rooms, day centres, nurseries and playgroups, hairdressers' salons and the host of other places. And many informants stressed a yet further role for transport: the simple need of the housebound to got out occasionally, to renew their experiences of city, shops, countryside and the larger world. But, as many Schemes have discovered, there is a major drawback to treating transport as a "neighbourly" activity: it is expensive. The question of who is to pay for what is a fundamental problem for all Good Neighbour Schemes, as they attempt to find a middle ground of neighbourliness between the welfare state and old-fashioned "charity"; we shall discuss the subject in detail in the next chapter.

Apart from visiting and transport, Schemes are engaged in, for example, doing odd jobs (258 respondents; 31 per cent), child-minding (128 respondents; 15 per cent) and making referrals to other organisations and agencies (182 respondents; 22 per cent). In addition, 71 per cent of our informants spoke of "other activities"; a vast range of specific kinds of help, support, care or advice for which they had discovered a need and which, in different ways, they were trying to satisfy. Although we found it difficult to classify these activities, we noted that they had one common characteristic (which applies equally to doing odd jobs and making referrals): they *make connections*. They link up private needs and public services, providing a safety net of information and contact for those who have fallen through the web of services provided by statutory and voluntary bodies, yet need care of a kind that Good Neighbour Schemes cannot themselves supply. This general function was frequently stressed by our informants: "we give emergency help until the statutory bodies can organise permanent assistance"; "we put those in need of help in touch with those offering help". The referral function illustrates how Good Neighbour Schemes can act as a "halfway house" between the two worlds of informal care, given by relations, neighbours and friends, and of formal care, provided by statutory social services. It was obvious to us that this role was clearly understood and valued by the organisers and members of Schemes; they said, for example, "we act as a clearing house for organisations in the city", or, "the Scheme is attempting to create a partnership between volunteers and statutory workers for the support and care of local people".

*Table 2*

*What are the Main Functions of the Scheme?*

| | | |
|---|---|---|
| Visiting | 632 | (76%) |
| Transport | 374 | (45%) |
| Odd jobs | 258 | (31%) |
| Referral to other organisations | 182 | (22%) |
| Child minding | 128 | (15%) |
| Other | 540 | (71%) |

Many respondents said that their Schemes did not engage in any specific activities but existed to "keep an eye on those at risk" or to help out in emergencies. Also, about 100 Schemes included the organising of social events and outings in their programme. Coffee mornings and luncheon clubs were both common methods of bringing people together, but by far

17

the most popular were the clubs that provided the elderly with some sort of day centre or rest room. Amongst the other clubs mentioned were junior youth clubs, single persons' clubs, arts and crafts clubs and keep fit groups.

Schemes also helped with children: some ran a crèche, one organised "a playweek for children during the summer holiday", and another undertook the tricky task of caring for children during a family crisis. "Granny sitting" also received a few mentions. Other respondents mentioned tasks that they undertook regularly; shopping and gardening were by far the most common. Many Schemes collect prescriptions for the elderly or housebound, but few collect pensions – perhaps because of the problems that might arise between the helper and the helped when money is involved. Certain types of personal service were also undertaken: for example, chiropody, "meals on wheels", and hairdressing; perhaps the most adventurous was a "victim support scheme – a crisis unit for the victims of crime".

Many Schemes also made qualitative comments about their work: for example, "we want to foster care between neighbours and others in the village", "we try to make neighbours aware of other neighbours' needs". These remarks are, once more, evidence of that general aim of promoting a "neighbourly" spirit that seems to lie at the heart of so many Good Neighbour Schemes. Some Schemes try to foster neighbourliness by, as one respondent put it, "helping newcomers to integrate into the community"; another informant said that "all newcomers are visited to see if they have any needs". One or two respondents had more ambitious goals, stating that their Schemes existed to look after "people's social and spiritual needs". Many others mentioned that they would "give any neighbourly help". Thus, in addition to building connections between Good Neighbours and those known, judged or admitting themselves to be in need, and between those in need and a variety of public services, about 40 per cent of the Schemes seem also to be involved in a *more general construction of social connections within the localities where they operate*. They are generating new social networks, especially self-help networks among those actually or potentially in need themselves. This is the whole point of putting so much energy into forming clubs, running day centres, organising outings, parties and other occasions or meetings, and becoming involved in baby-sitting pools, community or residents' associations, neighbourhood information shops, trouble-sharing discussion groups and a multitude of other attempts to foster mutual involvement among local residents. Over and above all this, the Schemes tend to become "dustbins" for miscellaneous urgent needs that the informal, voluntary and statutory systems of social care all find themselves unable to meet: dealing with prescriptions that doctors have been obliged to leave with housebound patients; emergency nursing of invalids or bathing and changing the disabled when the district nurse is too busy to turn up; tending the garden of an arthritic widow when the neighbours begin to complain that she is "letting the neighbourhood down"; getting a wasps' nest out of a chimney; changing library books. The diversity of tasks is enormous, but what it amounts to is the discovery of a range of needs to which family and neighbours, voluntary and statutory services cannot or do not respond effectively, whereas Good Neighbour Schemes can and do respond – perhaps because of their belief in the ideal of a more neighbourly society.

*Table 3*

*Whom does the Scheme serve?*

| | | |
|---|---|---|
| Elderly | 681 | (82%) |
| Housebound | 509 | (61%) |
| Handicapped | 366 | (44%) |
| Young families | 96 | (11%) |
| Single parents | 62 | ( 7%) |
| All ages | 159 | (19%) |

As Table 3 indicates, the largest client groups of Good Neighbour Schemes are: the elderly, with 681 mentions (82 per cent); the housebound, with 509 mentions (61 per cent); and the handicapped, with 366 mentions (44 per cent). These categories do, of course, overlap: many of the elderly will also be housebound and/or handicapped, and so forth. As with their range of activities, most Schemes insisted that they had no particular "target groups" of clients, but gave help wherever it was needed. Of those organised to help specific groups, 91 (11 per cent) helped only the elderly; two each helped the housebound and the handicapped; 96 regularly helped with young families; and 62 (7.5 per cent) helped single parents. We assume that most of the help given to these latter two groups consists of child-minding, although a few Schemes said that they encouraged self-help and mutual support activities in order to protect the interests of such groups in more general ways. Forty-two Schemes specifically listed child-minding among their functions and young families among their client groups, and 29 Schemes included child-minding and helping single parents. Although we have no detailed information about the kind of help given to these parents, it presumably extends well beyond the basics of child-minding and baby-sitting. One unusually explicit reply told us that the Scheme in question used these activities to draw "young parents into the life of the neighbourhood". In another case, a baby-sitting pool was described as a way of showing people "that we have all got something to give".

Only 22 replies (3 per cent) specifically mentioned attempts to combat loneliness: "we try to help the sad and lonely"; "we help lonely and poorly people". Yet it is obvious that many of the activities undertaken by the Schemes will have had the effect of reducing the isolation, if not the loneliness, of many people. Perhaps a characteristic of Good Neighbour

19

Schemes is that they concentrate on relatively practical tasks and do not overtly address more general problems – problems which may nevertheless be alleviated, and even solved, by the practical work they do. In some cases, this readiness to engage in practical efforts to meet all types of need, rather than to direct their activity towards a clear general goal, must cause problems for Good Neighbour Schemes. For example, seven Schemes apparently give help to "problem families", "families unable to cope", "families in crises" or "mothers with family problems". This area of need is certainly pressing, but it is debatable whether an organisation as informal and unskilled as a Good Neighbour Scheme can – or, indeed, should be expected to – provide help. A few Schemes said that they had been involved in "making a fuss to get welfare services of various kinds for people", thus demonstrating to the statutory authorities that organised neighbourhood care can have its aggressive side. Ten respondents said that they helped "the sick" and looked after people who were ill but who had nobody on hand. Almost one-fifth of Schemes (159 respondents) were ready to help 'all ages', and a considerable number said they would assist anybody in need. Clearly, many Schemes would offer help in any situation if they thought that they could cope; there were isolated instances of Schemes helping "people with personal problems and suicidal tendencies", ex-prisoners, ethnic minorities, the homeless, "inadequate people", "the socially deprived" and the bereaved. This diverse list of clients shows the remarkable willingness of Good Neighbour Schemes to tackle problems as they arise, as well as their readiness to expand their terms of reference whenever a new challenge presents itself. Indeed, one wonders whether there *are* any limits to that readiness; although we know a great deal about the help that Good Neighbour Schemes do give, we know nothing about the things they would definitely *not* do. There were one or two remarks about "deserving cases", but no mention of any specific boundaries to the terms of reference Schemes set themselves. Such boundaries must surely exist, but perhaps they have not yet been discovered.

The next major question we asked was about *the size of Good Neighbour Schemes*. We therefore enquired about the number of helpers and clients involved with each Scheme. Such a question does, unfortunately, overlook the fact that *many Schemes have an extremely unstable membership of both helpers and clients*. Accordingly, many respondents found difficulty in answering: 14 per cent were unable to give the number of helpers involved and 33 per cent could not state the number of clients helped. But it was clear from the replies we did receive that most Schemes were quite small: 241 (29 per cent) had fewer than 20 helpers, and 157 (19 per cent) had between 20 and 40. Even so, there were a few large Schemes: 109 (13 per cent) had between 41 and 80 helpers; 43 (5 per cent) had between 161 and 300; and 25 Schemes (3 per cent) had more than 301 helpers – a very large Scheme indeed. These figures must, however, be regarded with some caution. Many of our

20

informants were all too keenly aware of the difficulty of estimating the membership of a Scheme. The common pattern is for there to be a core of dedicated members who do a great deal of work, a periphery of helpers who are only occasionally involved, and then a "rump" of people who, having initially offered their services, either find that their enthusiasm has waned or that they cannot spare the time after all. Equally, of course, this last group could be seen as victims of bad management, who have simply not been drawn into the work of the Scheme when they should have been. Which of these views one takes will obviously affect one's judgement of whether such people should be considered as "genuine" members of the Scheme. Either way, they make it difficult to estimate accurately the size of almost all Schemes of this type.

Similar difficulties beset our attempts to discover precisely how many people receive help from a scheme. The more the scheme emphasises its informality, the more acute is the problem; especially where an attempt has been made to base the relationship between helpers and helped on reciprocity. We know of at least one scheme where the organiser tells those whom she thinks need help that they *could*, in turn, help the person assigned to them; it is thus hoped that a reciprocal relationship will develop, rather than a situation where one party gives and the other receives. In such cases, people obviously find it not only difficult but also unnecessary – and perhaps even wrong – to distinguish between helpers and helped. In much the same spirit, some informants said that they did not keep records of clients, because they considered them a threat to confidentiality.

Nevertheless, we were eventually able to make a broad estimate of how many people ("clients") were helped by the schemes. Of the 540 informants who felt able to put a number to those they helped, 161 said that they had fewer than 50 clients and 82 claimed between 51 and 100 clients. These figures probably indicate the number of clients being helped at the time our questionnaire was received, rather than the total number of people helped during the entire life of the schemes in question. Even on that basis, some schemes must represent a major source of care in their areas; 87 of them were helping between 101 and 300 people and 64 claimed more than 301 clients.

There seems to be some correlation between the number of helpers and the number of helped, since only 56 of the 243 schemes that had fewer than 100 clients had more than 40 helpers, whilst only 54 of the 151 schemes that claimed more than 101 clients had fewer than 40 helpers. Some replies claimed frankly amazing helper/client ratios: the extremes were 3 helpers to 1,100 clients and 450 helpers to 6 clients! There may well be incredibly efficient and hard-working people who can cover vast areas of need and, equally, some clients may be deluged with help from armies of helpers, but neither situation can be considered as reasonable or normal Good Neighbouring.

*Table 4*

*How many helpers are involved?*

| No. of Helpers | No. of Schemes | |
| --- | --- | --- |
| 0 – 20 | 241 | (34%) |
| 21 – 40 | 157 | (22%) |
| 41 – 80 | 139 | (19%) |
| 81 – 160 | 109 | (15%) |
| 161 – 300 | 43 | ( 6%) |
| More than 301 | 25 | ( 4%) |
| | N = 714 | (100%) |

*Table 5*

*How many clients are there?*

| No. of Clients | No. of Schemes | |
| --- | --- | --- |
| 0 – 50 | 161 | (30%) |
| 51 – 100 | 82 | (15%) |
| 101 – 300 | 87 | (16%) |
| More than 301 | 64 | (12%) |
| "whole area" | 146 | (27%) |
| | N = 540 | (100%) |

Our next questions concerned the payment of helpers and organisers and, more generally, the sources of finance for schemes. We found that the helpers and organisers of 678 schemes (82 per cent) were entirely unpaid, and that those of 135 schemes (16 per cent) were paid out-of-pocket expenses; only 6 schemes in our survey – less than 1 per cent – paid their helpers any sort of salary. Thus, *the vast majority of schemes depend entirely upon voluntary effort by the helpers.*

Furthermore, only a few schemes pay expenses, even though more than twice that number claim to provide transport and other expensive services for their clients; in all, 298 schemes that include transport among their functions make no payment to helpers and organisers. Some respondents even emphasised that helpers generally refused the offer of petrol money and would only accept payment for transport if the client insisted. Even so, it is rather hard to believe that so many people can afford to offer such expensive help without recompense, unless they do it so infrequently that the financial burden is negligible. Careful organisation can to some extent spread the load amongst helpers. But, even so, one is forced to conclude that Good Neighbour Schemes must appeal to a deep and genuine altruism in society – *or* that some members of the schemes are carrying quite disproportionate burdens for the sake of the ideal of neighbourhood care.

105 schemes (13 per cent) have a paid organiser and 3 schemes have a paid part-time secretary. We know that many organisers work full time without payment, but unfortunately we do not know how many. But we can at least be sure that 105 schemes have found the funds to pay for a full-time administrator. Where from? We found that 504 schemes (61 per cent) receive grants from an established statutory or voluntary body: 318 (38 per cent) from the local authority (mostly from the Social Services Department), 138 (17 per cent) from church organisations and 117 (14 per cent) from voluntary organisations. Some schemes receive grants from a combination of these agencies: 4 are funded from all three sources, 9 from the local authority and a church, 17 from the local authority and a voluntary organisation, and 11 from a church and a voluntary organisation. 150 schemes (18 per cent) receive donations from various private sources, and 183 schemes (22 per cent) undertook direct fund-raising.

But the critical statistic here is the number of schemes that receive money *solely* from donations and direct fund-raising; 35 schemes (4 per cent) survive financially only with the help of donations, and 72 schemes (8 per cent) through their own fund-raising activities; 26 (3 per cent) receive donations, engage in fund-raising, but receive no grant. And, furthermore, 219 schemes (26 per cent) exist without any source of income at all (or at least did not mention one). Obviously, a scheme with little or no money is restricted in what it can do: only 4 schemes financed exclusively by donations, and only 8 exclusively by their own fund-raising, managed to offer expenses to their helpers. Surprisingly, some schemes that do not receive a grant manage to pay an organiser: 2 schemes financed only by donations and 3 schemes financed only by their own efforts have succeeded in doing so.

On the question of who pays for the organisers – or rather, who provides finance for schemes with paid organisers – we found that 73 schemes with a grant from the local authority paid an organiser, as did 5 schemes with a grant from the church and 23 with a grant from a voluntary organisation.

In sum, it is clear that the funding of Good Neighbour Schemes is extremely modest – even though, to be effective, a scheme must obviously have some income. One or two schemes have persuaded the governmental authorities in their areas to treat them as "social experiments" or "demonstration projects" and have thus secured substantial grants (£1,000 or more per annum); without doubt, such schemes have flowered in a way that less fortunate schemes would dearly like to emulate. Yet our respondents were, in fact, somewhat ambivalent about funding. On the one hand, more money means more activity; but on the other, it can so often mean unwelcome entanglements with the organised social services. At the one extreme, a few schemes have accepted funding from local authorities within the framework of the Home Help Service; at the other, there are organisers who regard the fact that they receive no public money – and so escape any attachment to "the welfare" – as positively desirable, a measure of both independence and commitment. Some of our respondents said that a council grant would solve all their problems; others said that it would be the kiss of death. We shall return to this topic, where the crucial question seems once again to be: how to combine the effective provision of care with the promotion of "neighbourliness"?

*Table 6*

*Are the helpers paid and does the scheme have a paid organiser?*

| | | |
|---|---|---|
| Helpers unpaid | 678 | (82%) |
| Expenses for helpers | 135 | (16%) |
| Paid helpers | 6 | (0.7%) |
| Paid organiser | 105 | (13%) |
| Paid part-time secretary | 3 | (0.5%) |

*Table 7*

*What kind of financial support does the scheme receive?*

| | Exclusively | | All schemes | |
|---|---|---|---|---|
| Local authority grants | 198 | (24%) | 318 | (38%) |
| Church grants | 59 | ( 7%) | 138 | (16%) |
| Voluntary organisation grants | 41 | ( 5%) | 117 | (14%) |
| Donations | 35 | ( 4%) | 150 | (18%) |
| Direct fund-raising | 72 | ( 8%) | 183 | (22%) |
| None | | | 219 | (26%) |

The variations in size and the variety of financial support of schemes are matched by the diversity of their forms of organisation. Indeed, *were it not for their distinctive purpose of creating neighbourliness, it would be almost impossible to tell Good Neighbour Schemes apart from all the other caring projects based on voluntary visiting.* Diana Leat and Giles Darvill have suggested that voluntary visiting projects might be classified in terms of such criteria as: the range of help offered; the type of volunteers used; the type of visiting engaged in; the type of territorial and administrative arrangements adopted; the degree of formalisation of those arrangements; and the type of relationship that exists between the project and the statutory authorities. We looked at our 1026 Good Neighbour Schemes to see if they could be classified in those terms, only to find that, far from conforming to a single pattern, they display a thoroughly confusing mixture of every one of Leat and Darvill's criteria. So far as type of visiting is concerned, for example, it seems that Good Neighbour Schemes engage in "contact point" visiting, "check call" visiting, "emergency odd jobs" visiting, "routine odd jobs" visiting, "befriending" and visiting confined to particular client types – that is, *all* the kinds of visiting that Leat and Darvill had so helpfully distinguished.

When we tried to identify the ways in which schemes organised their activities the picture was almost as confused. We initially assumed that most schemes would simply have adopted administrative structures similar to the model constitution recommended by the National Council for Social Service in its pamphlet *Time to Care*. Alas, we were to discover (as did earlier case studies sponsored by The Volunteer Centre) that not only was every conceivable type of organisational arrangement to be found amongst Good Neighbour Schemes, but also that many schemes seem in a state of organisational flux for much of the time. Leat and Darvill distinguish five theoretical types of organisational structure: the "attached scheme"; the "street warden scheme"; the "community care scheme"; the "centralised visiting scheme"; and the "specialist scheme". Again, we found in practice that, despite an overall bias towards the "street warden" pattern, Good Neighbour Schemes offered examples of every one of these structures, and, moreover, that a majority of schemes embodied some mixture of them. Quite simply, *it is impossible to identify Good Neighbour Schemes as a distinct type of caring project on the basis of any single organisational principle.*

Must we then accept the sobering conclusion favoured by Leat and Darvill themselves, that Good Neighbouring is little more than a smart new name for a familiar, but perhaps slightly tarnished, form of social care – a public relations exercise rather than a genuinely new social experiment? Could it be true that "whether it is called volunteering or neighbouring is only relevant insofar as being called a volunteer puts people off"?

Despite all the diversity we have just catalogued, we do not agree. We prefer to emphasize two aspects of Good Neighbour Schemes that we feel make them more than just a "face-lift" for voluntary visiting. Firstly, much of their administrative diversity can be seen, on closer examination, to reflect a *tension between dispersal and centralisation* caused by the fact that the schemes are committed simultaneously to providing care *and* to promoting neighbourliness; we attempt to demonstrate the effects of this tension in the case studies presented later in this book. In general terms, the problem is one of maximising the devolved responsibilities of the "street-warden" pattern – the pattern most conducive to "neighbourliness" – while at the same time, in the interests of more effective delivery of care, exercising the co-ordination and control associated with the "centralised" and "attached" types of organisation. In practice, *the organisational diversity of Good Neighbour Schemes is not a symptom of chaos but a response to this tension in the light of local circumstances.*

Secondly, the commitment to neighbourliness, which causes much of the tension and the consequent organisational difficulties, is in the end regarded as paramount. Over 80 per cent of the informants who gave us "qualitative" reflections about their schemes stressed this view: "I think we would define our roles as caring, diagnostic, supportive, preventive and finally – and most important – involvement"; "It has been our aim to encourage a good

25

neighbour attitude in the village; that is what we put first"; "To sum up, then, we are a reciprocal service"; "Ideally, we don't have helpers and clients, just neighbours". Even when such explicit statements were lacking, our informants' descriptions of their schemes were almost always permeated by the same sense of the importance of neighbouring *in its own right*. One example must here speak for many hundreds:

> "The scheme's aim is to provide all local people with neighbourly help and care . . . To every 15–20 dwellings we have a person who is the 'Contact'. She is willing to be asked for help. She lives within the area of the dwellings that she cares for and so can keep an eye on her 'patch' easily. She does not do all the caring herself but encourages neighbours to look after each other. Some contacts put a great deal of time and effort into the work, some do the minimum. It is left up to the individual. If a situation arises they cannot cope with they seek help from statutory bodies, other contacts, the secretary or myself. Each estate covered has a 'leader' who is responsible for keeping contact alive on that estate, and that person is on a committee which meets about once a year. Organisation is kept to a minimum . . . We don't encourage contacts to report on what they do, we prefer it to be confidential, but we hear enough to be encouraged that it is well worth while."

In this context, whether a scheme is run by a committee or an organiser, whether it gets referrals from social workers, district nurses, street wardens or directly from residents, whether its "members" are all helpers or a mixture of helpers and helped, whether it has a centralised or dispersed organisational structure all seem to be of secondary importance. Organisation is adapted to local circumstances on the one hand and to the overriding goal of neighbourliness on the other. Indeed, it could be said that the distinctive principle of Good Neighbour Schemes is to use organisation to create a situation where organisation become unnecessary for the provision of social care.

## Origins and Relationships with the Statutory Services

In view of the uneasiness expressed by many of our informants about their relationships with the social services, we gave special attention to the question of the involvement of schemes with other voluntary and statutory agencies, in particular the Social Services Departments responsible for their districts. It would not be unreasonable to suppose that those relationships would have a major influence on the composition, organisation and activity of schemes. One might assume, for example, that schemes set up directly by Social Services Departments would have fewer difficulties with referrals than those initiated by local residents. Similarly, schemes lacking support from statutory agencies might be expected to have special problems of funding, service delivery and recruitment. But, surprisingly, the answers to our questions gave the lie to these and other such "commonsense" expectations.

Table 3 shows where the initiative for schemes came from. We were surprised to find that *by far the most common source of schemes is organised Christianity*. That the churches should be active in promoting neighbourliness is to be expected; the "good neighbour" is, after all, the type of the practising Christian. What we find remarkable is that the churches should play such an important role in a society where, on the one hand, religious observance seems to have suffered a drastic decline and where, on the other hand, efforts have been made by successive governments to foster organised neighbourliness on a strictly secular basis. Yet two-fifths of the schemes reported to us owed their existence to the church. Our category includes not only the main Christian denominations but also the various ecumenical and co-operative bodies that unite them; in fact, about half the church-originated schemes were the result of a joint effort between different denominations. Moreover, *60 per cent of church-initiated schemes had been in existence for more than five years* – a figure that contrasts dramatically with the 65 per cent of social services-initiated schemes that have come into being within the last five years. There seems to be a substantial religious basis to organised Good Neighbouring that, as yet, humanist and political sources have not been able to match.

*Table 8*

*Who initiated the scheme?*

| | | |
|---|---:|---|
| Churches | 323 | (39%) |
| Voluntary organisations | 227 | (27%) |
| Local residents | 136 | (16%) |
| Local authorities | 90 | (11%) |
| Parish councils | 17 | ( 2%) |
| Other | 37 | ( 5%) |

The second most frequently-mentioned source of schemes was national voluntary organisations, accounting for 27 per cent. Among these, *Age Concern was by far the most important,* followed at some distance by WRVS and then, at some distance again, by a scatter of other bodies that have sponsored experimental schemes in particular localities, very much as exceptions to their general pattern of activity. After the voluntary organisations, a not insignificant 16 per cent of schemes were initiated by local residents acting directly to generate neighbourhood care within their own localities. It is important to note that *many of these schemes are, in fact, offshoots of community, residents' or tenants' associations* – although almost a third of them (42 schemes) appear to have been launched by individuals, unsupported by any organ-

27

isation, who simply saw the need for neighbourhood care and felt able on their own initiative to get people together to do something about it. Very often – in every case, in fact, that we have been able to check – these individuals are *people with experience or training in nursing, social work or management – not simply Good Neighbours but qualified and competent Good Neighbours.* We think that such central figures are particularly important for the success of Good Neighbour Schemes and we shall come back to them later on. To sum up, then, it seems that, one way or another, 686 of the schemes surveyed (82 per cent) were initiated from outside the statutory welfare services – an impressive testimony to the vigour of voluntary and informal action independent of the workings of the state.

But the distinction is not quite as sharp as it appears. To begin with, local and national government has only recently begun to take direct action to initiate Good Neighbour Schemes, and its policies are still only exploratory in most parts of the country. Even so, if one examines the origins of schemes set up during the last two years, the contribution of the statutory authorities at 21 per cent (equal to that of local residents), is considerably more prominent than Table 8 seems to suggest. More to the point, perhaps, is the fact that the statutory services, even when they leave the initiation of schemes to others, do help those schemes to get started and do provide continuing support once they are in being.

Sixty-one per cent of schemes claim to have support from the social services; and in 36 per cent of cases, the social services provided considerable help (whether in the form of advice, information, publicity or cash) to schemes projected by others. In this respect, as Table 9 shows, voluntary organisations seem to do better than either local residents or the churches in obtaining help from the statutory services – possibly because they often have already-existing working relatioships with social workers and administrators, and possibly because some church and local residents' schemes seem to display a positive desire *not* to become entangled with the state. In any event, whereas 67 per cent of the schemes set up by voluntary organisations receive or have received support from the statutory services, only 55 per cent of those launched by local residents and 46 per cent of those launched by churches had been similarly blessed (or cursed!). Not surprisingly, 90 per cent of the schemes initiated by the social services also received support from them – indeed, one wonders what happens to the other 10 per cent! Social services involvement has, in other words, extended to every type of scheme, although not always even-handedly; it would certainly be valuable to know more than we do at the moment about the 333 schemes (40 per cent) that claim to have had no appreciable support from the statutory sector. Since, as we shall see, very few schemes list among their problems a lack of contact with the statutory services, one may assume that the 40 per cent of schemes which receive no support are not, in fact, suffering from isolation but have deliberately chosen independence.

*Table 9*

*Who initiated the Scheme?*

| | Social Services helped to set up the Scheme | Support received from the Social Services | |
|---|---|---|---|
| Church | 71 | 156 | (46%) |
| Voluntary organisation | 85 | 150 | (67%) |
| Local residents | 43 | 75 | (55%) |
| Local authority | 82 | 82 | (90%) |
| Parish council | 5 | 10 | (60%) |

The presence or absence of support from statutory agencies does not, however, seem to make a dramatic difference to the actual functioning of schemes. Not surprisingly, schemes initiated by the Social Services and other statutory bodies devote significantly more effort to making referrals to other agencies (presumably the Social Services) than do schemes orginating from other sources. Conversely, they do least in the way of providing transport; this is less easy to understand, but it might mean that they are referring requests for transport to other organisations. It could also reflect the social composition of this type of scheme. Support for this interpretation is perhaps provided by the fact that church-initiated schemes are the most active of all in providing transport – probably because their membership includes a high proportion of people who can afford to pay the cost of providing such a service from their own pockets.

The aspect of statutory sponsorship that has the greatest significance for the survival and success of schemes is, perhaps predictably, the availability of funds. *Schemes initiated by statutory bodies are much more likely than other types of scheme to have both paid organisers and provision for paying members' out-of-pocket expenses.* They are, in fact, twice as likely to enjoy these benefits as schemes launched by churches or local residents. And the same pattern appears, although less marked, where local authority grants are concerned; 60 per cent of these schemes receive such grants, compared with only 41 per cent of schemes launched by local residents and 31 per cent of the church-initiated schemes. In more general terms, the financial support for schemes follows a predictable pattern. Each type of scheme is most likely to receive aid from the most immediate and appropriate sponsor: local authority money goes disproportionately to local authority schemes, church money to church schemes, and voluntary organisation money to voluntary organisation schemes; and schemes launched by local residents are disproportionately dependent on donations and direct fund-raising. The origins and affiliations of schemes have certain other, predictable effects on their functioning, none of which is important enough, however, materially

29

to alter their distinctive common purpose. *Thus, church-based schemes tend to have more helpers and a better helper/client ratio than other types of scheme* – although it is not clear whether this is because they can recruit helpers from entire congregations, or simply because they have usually been in existence for longer than other types of scheme. Schemes promoted by voluntary organisations are more likely than others to devote themselves to helping the elderly – surely a consequence of the special efforts of Age Concern in encouraging Good Neighbour Schemes. It is less clear why church-originated schemes should be more than twice as likely as any other type to be involved in helping young families – although, once again, this may be an example of the make-up of the "congregation" determining how schemes actually operate. Finally, 48 per cent of schemes initiated by local residents (and by Parish Councils) operate in rural, as distinct from urban or surburban, settings compared with 25 per cent of schemes launched by other sources; as we shall see later, the members of residents' schemes often claim that much of what they do would be done by local people anyway, since "this is a very neighbourly place".

## Regional Variations

A further aim of our survey was to discover how Good Neighbour Schemes were distributed throughout the country. Accordingly, we have classified the replies on the basis of the standard regional categories devised by the DHSS. We have tried to show both the overall geographical distribution of schemes and the incidence of specific types of scheme in certain areas.

*Table 10*

| Regional Distribution of Good Neighbour Schemes | | |
|---|---|---|
| North | 53 | (6%) |
| North West | 109 | (13%) |
| Yorkshire/Humberside | 77 | (9%) |
| West Midlands | 68 | (8%) |
| East Midlands | 49 | (6%) |
| East Anglia | 31 | (4%) |
| South West | 100 | (11%) |
| South East | 343 | (43%) |

At first sight, these figures suggest that there is a massive concentration of schemes in one region and that, in at least three others, they are remarkably scarce. But if we compare the distribution of schemes with the distribution of the population as a whole, the regional discrepancies almost disappear. Indeed, as Table 11 shows, all we are left with is a slight proportional over-representation in the South East and South West, and a slight under-representation elsewhere.

30

*Table 11*

Regional Distribution of Schemes and of the General Population

| Region | % of Schemes | % of Population |
|---|---|---|
| North | 6 | 7 |
| North West | 13 | 14 |
| Yorkshire/Humberside | 9 | 11 |
| West Midlands | 8 | 11 |
| East Anglia | 4 | 4 |
| South West | 11 | 9 |
| South East | 43 | 37 |

A more significant indicator, however, is the *incidence of schemes in relation to a region's presumed need for the kinds of social care that Good Neighbour Schemes distinctively seek to meet*. In the absence of any simple statistics that would demonstrate this relationship, we had to construct a rather complicated table of our own. For each region, we took three general indices of social deprivation (the take-up of unemployment benefit; the proportion of people living solely on welfare benefits; the average weekly household income) and five more specific indices that we felt pointed to the existence of the types of need that Good Neighbour Schemes can typically meet (numbers of handicapped people; numbers of old age pensioners living alone; numbers of single-parent families living on their own; numbers of households without cars and telephone; numbers of household receiving Home Help services). In each case, we calculated these figures as a proportion of the total regional population, then placed the regions in rank order. We then amalgamated the columns of figures to produce a composite indicator of the regional distribution of "the need for social care". Finally, we related this to the regional distribution of Good Neighbour Schemes proportionate to population. Table 12 is the result of this exercise; a glance at columns 9 and 10 in particular will show that the impression given by Table 10 of a *dramatic regional maldistribution of Schemes* is now, in fact, reinforced.

The picture has now become rather complicated. Although it is clear that the regions with the lowest levels of need, the South East and South West, enjoy best provision of social care from Good Neighbour Schemes, the reverse is by no means the case. The North and North East, the regions with the highest levels of need, certainly have far fewer schemes than the South East and South West, but they are not the most deprived regions in that respect. Rather, it is Yorkshire and the Midlands, in the middle range of need, that seem to have the lowest incidence of Good Neighbour Schemes. We shall try to account for this slightly puzzling situation later in the book. But first we shall look at each region in turn and briefly describe the nature of the schemes it contains.

The *Northern Region* comprises the counties of Tyne and Wear, Cleveland, Cumbria, Durham and Northumberland. Its main urban areas are to the

*Table 12*

Ranking of Regions According to Incidence of Needs and
Incidence of Good Neighbour Schemes*

| | GENERAL DEPRIVATION | | | | | | SPECIFIC NEEDS | | | |
|---|---|---|---|---|---|---|---|---|---|---|
| | 1 | 2 | 3 | 4 | 5 | 6 | 7 | 8 | 9 | 10 |
| | Unemployment benefit | Other welfare benefits | Weekly household income | Handicapped | O.A.P.'s living alone | Single parents on own | Households without car or telephone | Households receiving Home Help Services | Overall Need | Good Neighbour Schemes |
| **REGION** | | | | | | | | | | |
| North | 2 | 1 | 1 | 2 | 3 | 1 | 1 | 2 | 1 | 5 |
| North West | 1 | 3 | 4 | 1 | 1 | 2 | 4 | 3 | 2 | 4 |
| Yorks/Humberside | 4 | 2 | 2 | 3 | 2 | 3 | 2 | 1 | 3 | 7 |
| West Midlands | 3 | 6 | 7 | 5 | 8 | 5 | 3 | 5 | 4 | 8 |
| East Midlands | 5 | 5 | 5 | 6 | 7 | 6 | 5 | 4 | 5 | 6 |
| East Anglia | 6 | 4 | 3 | 7 | 5 | 8 | 6 | 8 | 6 | 3 |
| South West | 7 | 7 | 6 | 4 | 6 | 7 | 7 | 7 | 7 | 2 |
| South East | 8 | 8 | 8 | 8 | 4 | 4 | 8 | 6 | 8 | 1 |

\* 1 = highest incidence : 8 = lowest incidence. Rankings are calculated in
terms of incidence relative to regional population.

north-east, on the banks of the Rivers Tyne, Wear and Tees, and to the
north-west is the Lake District. Northumberland and Cumberland are
predominantly rural, whilst Durham County is a curious mixture of rural
areas and mining villages. The region has 53 Good Neighbour Schemes (6
per cent of the total for England), most of which are in urban or suburban
settings and very few in rural areas. Most of the schemes were set up within
the last 5 years; there is proportionately the largest number of schemes of
any region (34 per cent) set up between 1 and 2 years ago. The chief
initiators of schemes in the Northern Region have been voluntary organisations, who set up 19 schemes (36 per cent). The area seems well-served
by organised voluntary groups such as Age Concern and the WRVS;
Northumberland Age Concern alone has more than 1000 helpers on its
books. The Social Services maintain contact with most of the schemes in the
area; they helped to set up 29 of them (55 per cent) and provide support to
37 (70 per cent).

Visiting is by far the most usual function of these schemes; only a few mentioned transport and doing odd jobs. The elderly, the housebound and the handicapped were the most commonly-helped client groups. The vast majority of schemes have unpaid helpers; only 5 schemes (9 per cent) provide expenses. There is one paid scheme and, surprisingly, 13 schemes with a paid organiser. This high proportion of paid organisers is probably the result of the number of schemes initiated by voluntary organisations, and of the extensive involvement of Social Services (see Table 11). Most schemes are small: the majority have few than 20 helpers and 50 clients. Two-fifths of the schemes receive no financial support; otherwise, the most important source of finance is local authority grants, received by 21 schemes.

The *North West Region* includes the counties of Cheshire and Lancashire and the two large conurbations of Greater Manchester and Merseyside. We received information about 109 schemes in this region (13 per cent of the national total). Most were in urban or suburban settings (27 in Greater Manchester and 10 in Merseyside), leaving 32 per cent in rural settings. Only a small number of schemes in this region originated within the last two years, most having been set up either 2 – 5 years ago or more than five years ago (83 per cent in the North West compared with 62 per cent in the North). As in the Northern Region, voluntary organisations were the most usual initiators, responsible for 44 schemes (40 per cent), although the churches (27 per cent) are somewhat more in evidence in this region. Once again, the Social Services maintain contact with a majority of schemes, having helped to set up 46 (42 per cent) and providing support to 77 (71 per cent); the Social Services Departments in Greater Manchester give support to 24 of the 27 schemes in their area. Schemes in the North West seem rather more diverse in their functions than those in the North – apart from the usual high incidence of visiting services, many schemes make referrals to other organisations, provide transport and do odd jobs. Once again, the elderly, the housebound and the handicapped were by far the most common client groups. In the North West, schemes are more likely to have paid organisers than in any other region, and there is also the largest proportion of schemes (22 per cent) that offer expenses to their helpers. The region has two fully-paid schemes, one of which pays workers via the Manpower Services Commission. Many of the schemes were quite large: over 20 per cent of those who answered the relevant question reported more than 80 helpers, and over 30 per cent of those who specified the number of clients reported more than 100. A local authority grant was the most common source of finance, received by 53 schemes (49 per cent), although many schemes rasied money in more informal ways by accepting donations and by direct fund raising.

*Yorkshire and Humberside* includes North, South and East Yorkshire and Humberside. The northern part of the region is mostly rural, but there are three major industrial areas: Humberside; Leeds and its surrounding towns in West Yorkshire; Sheffield and its neighbouring towns in South Yorkshire. We had replies from 77 schemes (9 per cent of the national total) in this region, 43 of them from the Leeds and West Yorkshire area; 74 per cent were in urban or suburban settings. Most of these schemes were set up more than five years ago; only ten have been launched in the last two years. Nearly half the schemes were set up by the churches (including 21 of those in Leeds and West Yorkshire), and 23 were launched by voluntary organisations. Although only 7 schemes were actually initiated by local authorities, Social Services Departments had helped to set up 31 (40 per cent) and were giving support to 46 (60 per cent); quite a high degree of Social Service involvement compared with other regions. More than half the schemes provide transport, and 47 per cent do odd jobs – the highest percentage in any region. There is also an exceptionally large number of schemes that engage in child-minding and helping young families. Although the majority of the schemes are unpaid, the region has an above-average proportion of schemes that offer expenses to helpers. Most of the schemes that answered our question about the number of helpers appeared to be fairly small, having fewer than 40 helpers, but there were several schemes represented in each of our size categories. In terms of the number of clients, there was a similar spread: 30 per cent had under 50 clients, whilst at the other extreme 30 per cent claimed to serve "the whole area" in which they operated (27 per cent certainly had more than 100 clients). A further 14 schemes were described as serving "all ages", implying that any request for help would be dealt with. Twenty-six schemes receive no financial support; for the remainder, the major source of grants is either the local authority or a church.

The *West Midlands* consists of the counties of Herefordshire and Worcestershire, Salop, Staffordshire, Warwickshire and the West Midlands. It includes the heavily industrial West Midland area and the "Potteries", the conurbation centred on Stoke. Sixty-eight schemes (8 per cent of the total for England) from this region replied to our questionnaire, 50 from urban or suburban areas (of which 19 were from Birmingham and the West Midlands) and 18 from rural areas. Only 10 per cent of these schemes were set up within the last two years; the remainder were divided equally between those launched between two to five years ago and those launched over five years ago. The schemes in the region were mainly initiated, in more or less equal numbers, by voluntary organisations, by churches or by local residents not acting on behalf of any outside body. Social Services involvement was reasonably widespread; Departments had helped to set up 23 schemes (34 per cent) and supported 43 (63 per cent). The schemes were mainly engaged in visiting the elderly, the housebound and the handicapped, although 20 schemes provided transport and 36 did odd jobs. These schemes are mostly unpaid; only 8 offer expenses to their helpers and only 5 have paid organisers. The majority of schemes in the region are small: 69 per cent have fewer than 40 helpers and 40 per cent have fewer than 50 clients, although the remainder are spread fairly evenly throughout the categories of helper and client numbers. Most schemes in the West Midlands receive some financial support; local authorities give grants to 43 per cent of them and, for some reason not clear to us, schemes in the area receive appreciably more income from donations than those in any other region.

The *East Midlands* comprises the counties of Derbyshire, Leicestershire, Lincolnshire, Northamptonshire and Nottinghamshire; in each case, the county town is a sizeable urban area. A majority of the 49 schemes in the region operate in these urban areas, and most were set up more than 5 years ago. As in the West Midlands, the major initiators of Good Neighbour Schemes were the churches, the voluntary organisations and the local residents, who between them accounted for 81 per cent. Local authority involvement was comparatively slight; they initiated only 4 schemes, helped set up only 16 and gave support to only 28 (57 per cent). Few schemes were involved in odd jobs or childminding, yet there was the highest percentage for any region engaged in visiting—accordingly, the elderly were the most common client group, but no respondents mentioned helping single parents and only 2 mentioned helping young families. Nearly half the schemes had fewer than 40 helpers, but the median range had 41-80 helpers. Most of the respondents who answered the question about client numbers said that their schemes had fewer than 100 helpers, although 25 per cent claimed over 100. Eighty-eight per cent of schemes in the East Midlands enjoy some financial support and over half receive a local authority grant – the highest proportion in the country.

*East Anglia* consists of the mainly rural counties of Cambridgeshire, Norfolk and Suffolk; the 31 replies from this region were almost equally distributed between urban/suburban and rural settings. One-third of the schemes reported to us were set up during the last five years. The chief initiators of schemes were the churches, responsible for 35 per cent, and local residents, responsible for 26 per cent – marginally more than in any other region. East Anglia has England's lowest reported percentage of schemes set up or supported by the Social Services; 23 and 50 per cent respectively. A comparatively high proportion of schemes offer transport – perhaps the result of the predominantly rural nature of the region. Ninety per cent of schemes in East Anglia are unpaid and – surprisingly, in view of the number of schemes providing transport – only 2 offer expenses to their helpers. There are, however, 6 paid organisers, together with one of the 6 fully-paid schemes about which we have information. The size of these schemes varies considerably: 53 per cent have fewer than 40 helpers and only 6 respondents claimed more than 80 helpers or 80 clients. Nearly all schemes in East Anglia receive some financial support, chiefly from local authority grants, donations or their own fund-raising.

The *South West* region comprises the predominantly rural counties of Devon, Dorset, Gloucestershire, Somerset and Wiltshire; accordingly, 55 of the 100 schemes reported from the area operate in rural settings. Over half these schemes were set up more than 5 years ago. The chief initiators have been the churches (33 per cent) and voluntary organisations (35 per cent). Comparatively few schemes in rural areas seem to enjoy contact with their local Social Service Departments; East Anglia and the South West, the two most rural regions, have the worst record in the country.

Compared with East Anglia, however, proportionately more schemes in the South West received help from Social Services when starting up (37 per cent), and about the same proportion (51 per cent) enjoyed continuing support from that source. Most schemes in the region engage in visiting and a sizeable number make referrals to other agencies and provide transport. The majority of respondents named the elderly as their major client group, and 27 per cent said that they would help all ages. Eighty-nine per cent of schemes in the South West are unpaid; there was only one fully-paid scheme, 4 with paid organisers and 9 that offered expenses to their helpers. The schemes vary considerably in size; the most usual number of helpers is 41 – 80 (31 per cent), although 51 per cent of the relevant replies claimed fewer than 40 helpers. There was also considerable variation in the number of clients, although 31 per cent of schemes were described as serving the whole area. Despite the small number of schemes that had links with their local Social Services Departments, we found that the most common source of finance in this region was local authority grants.

The final region, the *South East,* includes Greater London and the counties of Bedfordshire, Berkshire, Buckinghamshire, Essex, Hampshire, Hertfordshire, Isle of Wight, Kent, Oxfordshire, Surrey and East and West Sussex. This region is dramatically different from all others. It has the highest concentration of Good Neighbour Schemes: 343, or 43 per cent of the total. Even though the region includes Greater London, from which we received 99 replies, the remaining 11 counties have 240 schemes – almost a third of all those in England. The peculiar character of the region is best illustrated by the 249 schemes that operate in urban or suburban settings, many of them in the suburbs that have spread out from London but which are heavily influenced by surrounding rural towns and villages, producing a distinctive "quasi-rural suburbanism". Half the schemes in the South East were set up more than 5 years ago and, since then, there has been a fairly steady growth: an average of 37 schemes were set up per year in the "2 – 5 years ago" category, and 38 schemes per year were set up 1 – 2 years ago. Since the South East has many more schemes than any other region, it is almost inevitable that it should also take the lead in the number of schemes initiated by specific sources; in particular, 53 per cent of all schemes set up by the churches and 60 per cent of all those started by local residents. Within the region itself, however, we discovered that the churches are by far the most common originators of schemes, being responsible for 50 per cent of the total. At first sight, the figures for statutory involvement are quite impressive: the local authority set up 32 schemes, whilst Social Services set up 114 schemes and provide support to 202. Yet these amount to little over half the total; some 41 per cent of the region's schemes appear to exist without any support from Social Services. The Good Neighbour Schemes of the South East exhibit considerable variety both in their functions and in their client groups; for example, no fewer than 56 per cent provide transport, whilst 20 per cent offer child-minding, the highest proportion of any region. Although the region has no fully-paid schemes, 69 schemes (20 per cent) pay expenses and 47 have a paid organiser; but in 79 per cent the helpers are unpaid. There is equal diversity in the size of schemes, with every category of complement of helpers and clients represented by a fair number of schemes. There are, however, appreciably more large and very large schemes than in any other region: 16 per cent (38 schemes) were reported as having more than 300 clients, whilst 32 per cent were said to have more than 80 helpers and 11 per cent more than 160 – in each case, these percentages are the highest for any region. We at first thought that most of these large schemes would be in Greater London, but in fact that area has only 2 schemes with more than 300 helpers and only 15 with more than 300 clients. Throughout the South East, 130 schemes receive a grant from the local authority; but, surprisingly, only 71 of the 170 schemes initiated by the churches said that they received a church grant.

It is ironic that the South East, even excluding Greater London, should have such a large proportion of England's Good Neighbour Schemes. Although the Home Counties and their neighbours cover a large area, the region is well known to be the most affluent in the country. This is not to say, however, that social need does not exist; the problems of the elderly, the handicapped, the housebound and young families are no less pressing within an affluent milieu, and there are, moreover, many poor people living in the region. But, as we have already shown, there is certainly *proportionately* less need than in the more "deprived" regions such as the North East or North West.

This disconcerting concentration of Good Neighbouring in the area where it is apparently least needed can, we suggest, be explained by the fact that the *incidence of schemes does not reflect the level of need in a given environment but rather the availability of helpers and organisers*. Although our information does not permit a precise quantitative analysis of the social composition of schemes, it seems clear that *schemes develop most readily in areas where there is a large supply of people (mainly women) who not only do not do full-time work but can also afford to meet the costs involved in being a Good Neighbour*. It is no accident that one of the commonest explanations given for the breakdown of "natural neighbourliness" in modern society is that nowadays so many more women go out to work, and thus do not have the time to form the neighbourly relationships they used to do – nor, presumably, the time to join neighbourhood care schemes either. Thus it seems that *Good Neighbour Schemes – at least those based on the minimal levels of funding and payment that are now standard – flourish not where the need for care is greatest, but where need and a certain level of prosperity exist side by side –* compare the 32 per cent of schemes with more than 80 helpers in the South East with the mere 7 per cent of schemes of similar size in the North.

Clearly, one major problem for Good Neighbour Schemes is how to introduce their distinctive formula for social care into areas and populations that lack the specific social characteristics of the South East. Table 13 indicates the problem – and perhaps suggests a solution. The South East, as demonstrated in Table 12, enjoys both the lowest level of need and the highest incidence of Good Neighbour Schemes. The North, by contrast, has the highest level of need – but it is nevertheless reasonably well provided with schemes. It may well be that traditional claims about the greater "friendliness" of people in the North are true, and are reflected in the relatively high incidence of schemes; but, that apart, the explanation suggested by Table 13 is plain enough. Good Neighbour Schemes in the South East are, relatively speaking, independent of the state and dependent upon private prosperity. By contrast, the fact that the North is not at the bottom of the regional league table for Good Neighbour Schemes is perhaps largely the result of the relatively active role of statutory authorities in that region in promoting, supporting and funding schemes, as a positive alternative to the assumption that, in the face of growing social need, they will develop 'naturally'. If this interpretation is correct, it would obviously be quite wrong to think of Good Neighbour Schemes as simply an alternative to the welfare state. Rather, if such schemes are to provide social care where it is most needed, they can do so only in active co-operation with the welfare state.

*Table 13*

*Relation with Statutory Agencies*

|  | North | South East |
|---|---|---|
| Social Services initiated the scheme | 15% | 9% |
| Social Services helped initiate the scheme | 55% | 33% |
| Social Services support the scheme | 70% | 59% |
| The scheme has a paid organiser | 25% | 14% |

# III
# Problems and Successes

Fifty-eight per cent of our informants said that their schemes had "major problems" of one sort or another, and 71 per cent said that their schemes "could be more successful". In this section we shall look at the various problems schemes seem to face and at the measures which their organisers believe would make them more successful. Some of the broad categories of problem and solution are presented in Table 14 and 15: it will be noticed that the two sets of answers mirror one another closely.

*Table 14*

| Problem | *Major Problems of Good Neighbour Schemes* Percentage of Schemes (N = 483) |
|---|---|
| Shortage of helpers | 43% |
| Inappropriate helpers | 21% |
| Transport difficulties | 20% |
| Organisation/administration | 19% |
| Inadequate contact with external agencies (Social Services etc.) | 19% |
| Shortage of clients | 15% |
| Shortage of finance | 14% |
| Other | 29% |

By far the most commonly-reported problem was a shortage of helpers; and by far the most frequently-mentioned prescription for greater success was more helpers. This is hardly surprising, of course – although we were interested to note that, while a shortage of helpers is a problem for schemes of all types, those initiated by statutory authorities seemed significantly more prone to suffer from it (one in three) that those initiated by local residents or churches (rather less than one in four). Similarly, this problem seemed more frequently to afflict schemes with paid organisers than those with unpaid organisers. These differences may tell us more about the expectations of organisers who are paid or work closely with the statutory authorities than they do about the actual availability of helpers. But what does seem clear is that *for all types of scheme the difficulty of recruiting Good*

*Neighbours is a paramount concern.* Indeed, Table 14 almost certainly under-estimates the size of the problem, since many of the replies grouped under the heading of "Other" did in fact refer to such things as "women going out to work", "finding replacements for helpers who leave the area", "public apathy", "difficulty of persuading helpers to do certain tasks that are needed", "difficulty of getting helpers to work in certain areas (such as council estates or tower blocks)" – all of which could also be interpreted as pointing to an inadequate supply of Good Neighbours.

*Table 15*

*Factors that would make Good Neighbour*
*Schemes more successful*

| Factor | Percentage of Schemes (N = 590) |
|---|---|
| More helpers | 44% |
| Different helpers | 28% |
| More finance | 19% |
| Better contact with Social Services etc. | 14% |
| Paid organiser | 11% |
| More clients | 11% |
| Other | 54% |

Within the overall problem of the shortage of helpers, a number of specific issues stand out. Thus, 21 per cent of our informants identified the problem as a matter of *finding helpers "of the right type"*. In practice, this can mean many different things. Sometimes it is a case of finding the "right people to do the jobs at the right time". Sometimes respondents are much more specific: "We've had a lot of old ladies volunteering, but unfortunately most of the help people ask for needs someone strong and energetic"; "Most of our helpers live in a middle-class street which isn't much use as most of the referrals are right over in a working-class area"; "Many who volunteer in a moment of generosity are not available when you really need them"; or, more bluntly, "We had a lot of quite unsuitable people volunteering when we first began". The constant variations on this theme are, in our view, not so much a criticism of the people who volunteer as Good Neighbours but more an indication of the real problems many schemes face in matching the help they can offer to the need for social care that exists in their particular localities.

In order to discover and meet local needs effectively, schemes may need to be able to mobilise *two quite distinct types of effort,* and perhaps to call on the services of two quite distinct types of Good Neighbour. First, they need a large number of people willing and able to carry out *monitoring* within highly localised areas: local residents who can 'drop in' regularly and easily or who can unobtrusively but comprehensively keep an eye on those living around them. This requires the building-up of a sound body of local information effective in discovering need and in providing and maintaining contact between those in need and those who can provide care. But, secondly, in so far as schemes seek to provide care themselves, they also need people willing and able to take on *specific caring tasks,* often of a fairly strenuous nature, or to guarantee to provide particular services (such as cleaning, gardening, shopping, reading, driving) with strict reliability and regularity.

Ideally, no doubt, the two types of task should be performed by the same people. But, in practice, the roles seem to drift apart. Monitoring is essential but fairly unrewarding; it can easily win one the reputation of being nosy rather than helpful. It tends to be unstructured, informal and comprehensive in its demands. Doing it well calls for genuine qualities of neighbourliness – and, at the same time, the willingness frequently to spend a great deal of time apparently doing nothing. *The essence of the job is just being there, being trusted and being in touch.* It is often difficult to tell an inquirer just what one is doing. By contrast, the second type of work involves very clearly recognised activities. It is sharply-defined and relatively formal; the demands are exacting but limited. This type of Good Neighbouring leans towards the provision of service, whereas the first type leans towards the cultivation of neighbourliness. The second category of Good neighbour usually has no difficulty in describing his or her "neighbourly" activities.

The problem of the supply of Good Neighbours is, at bottom, largely a matter of *arranging an appropriate match between the kinds of people available to schemes as helpers and the need to perform these two rather different types of work within the locality.* Case studies 1 and 2 in the next chapter both illustrate this dilemma. On the one hand, it is necessary to sustain the morale of people who find that a scheme apparently gives them little to do, and on the other it is necessary to find people with sufficient time, resources and commitment to take on the tasks that the organisers find waiting to be done.

Skilful management is needed to meet both demands simultaneously. In some of the schemes that we judged most successful (case study 6, for example) the organisers had clearly devoted equal amounts of effort to both problems, even to the extent of stressing the primary importance of recruiting and sustaining street monitors or contact-people. But the overall tendency among those informants who saw the supply of helpers as a major problem was to concentrate on recruiting the more active type of helper – thus, perhaps, giving their scheme an underlying bias towards the delivery of services rather than the cultivation of neighbourliness. As respondent after respondent put it, from that point of view *"quality rather than quantity is needed"*. Thus: "there is always a shortage of volunteers for long-term help"; "there are just not enough people you can count on to undertake regular visiting on a long-term basis"; "they are unwilling to commit themselves";

"they resist organisation"; or "plenty of people say they want to help until you tell them just what help you want them to give". Superficially, it could be said that such problems *arise from a discrepancy between the services organisers would like their schemes to provide and the help that volunteer Good Neighbours are able to offer.*

But we feel there is more to it than that: there is, in our view, a discrepancy between what people can objectively get out of working for a Good Neighbour Scheme and what the people who offer to work for such schemes are subjectively looking for. In a separate study we have found that, although people join Good Neighbour Schemes for many reasons, there are two principal concerns. *The overriding motive of the Good Neighbour is to be more closely involved with others.* Social care is seen as a basis for such involvement. *But, for some people, giving care then becomes the paramount consideration, while for others neighbourly contacts and relationships as such are what ultimately matter.* These two concerns do, of course, echo the twin objectives of Good Neighbour Schemes. But, once again, we find that in practice they easily become separated from one another. The provision of social care can all too easily be pursued without regard for – and perhaps even at the expense of – the cultivation of neighbourliness. Paradoxically, the problem of the shortage of helpers, or of the wastage of helpers, or of the dearth of helpers of the "right type", in Good Neighbour Schemes seems largely to arise from the fact that schemes have no easy recipe for building the rewards of neighbourliness into their activities and that, in response to *the immediate pressure to provide caring services, they tend to move towards a more traditional voluntary service type of activity and organisation.* As our fifth case study amply demonstrates, there is a tension between the two aims of Good Neighbour Schemes that many schemes seem able to cope with only by severely subordinating one aim to the other.

Thus, many schemes faced with this problem have tried to solve it by concentrating the work that comes their way in the hands of a "core group" of volunteers closely in touch with the organiser. Although this may well bring about strong relationships within the core group, it also poses a threat to a more widespread neighbourhood involvement. The concept of a Good Neighbour network gives way to something like a highly organised local task-force for service delivery. The logic of the shift is hard to resist. As one organiser put it: "If a case is referred to me I want to deal with it at once – that means going to someone I can count on, not hunting around for someone who happens to live near the case".

Interestingly, schemes initiated by statutory agencies and schemes with paid organisers seem especially prone to develop in this particular direction. Although the organisers of several such schemes told us that they had difficulty in convincing local residents that they were genuinely independent of the welfare state – in other words, that they were interested in neighbourliness rather than simply the provision of services – it was particularly among these schemes that the tendency towards the task-force model was most evident. Once again, the reasoning is understandable: "obviously a scheme that is imposed on the community does not receive as much support as one that comes from within it"; "our workers find it difficult to find volunteers to help out – it is difficult to break down the distrust of anybody associated with officialdom"; "unfortunately the local people have proved very unreliable when it comes to organising things – luckily, the Job Creation workers have meant that we can carry on without them"; "we hoped to be able to get a group of local people to take over, but in fact that hasn't happened, and we've had to rely more on the full-time workers and a handful of the original members of the committee"; and most explicitly, "in the long term we would like to make this a more neighbourly place, but right now getting people to and from hospital takes all our strength". Such comments raise the whole question of the proper relationship between Good Neighbour Schemes and the statutory authorities in a direct and quite uncomfortable way. But before taking up that theme, and the related theme of the internal organisation and administration of schemes, we should say something about the second most common "major problem" reported by our informants – the provision of transport.

In one sense, the *problem of transport* is another aspect of the problem of the supply of helpers; it is a matter of finding the kind of Good Neighbours who are willing and able to provide transport largely free of charge. And this, in turn, is but another aspect of the problem of matching care to need. One or two schemes have received grants or donations towards the cost of transport, and their effect on activity and morale were reported to us enthusiastically: "Having the minibus has made so much difference – we've got lots of drivers now and most of the passengers contribute to the petrol. It's become our symbol". But the vast majority of schemes find themselves fending off a stream of requests for transport because they have neither vehicles nor drivers. We were told of a number of schemes that had collapsed altogether because of their inability to meet local needs for transport. We suggested in the last chapter that an important prerequisite for Good Neighbouring seems to be the coexistence in a locality of social need and a certain level of prosperity. In fact, many of the comments we received about transport problems pointed quite specifically at this "social" basis of Good Neighbouring: "The scheme has folded as a result of the recent squeeze, which has meant that any woman who can has got a job and is just not available to help"; "not many people who are around during the day have a car (because of the rise in car-tax many people have given up their second car) so there is no-one to call on for transport".

Whatever one thinks of the social implications of such statements, there is no doubt that an essential element in Good Neighbouring is the creation of neighbourly relationships between local residents who were previously strangers. Nor is there any doubt that such relationships cannot be cultivated simply by "throwing people together". *The best prospect for creating neighbour-*

43

*liness is unquestionably to enable people to get to know one another in the context of specific tasks and acts of help.* Providing transport is ideal for this purpose. It is an occasion for people to meet that permits close contact yet is not intrusive; in effect, a reasonable and unthreatening basis on which to explore the possiblity of building up a relationship. We feel, therefore, that the organisers of schemes are absolutely correct in seeing transport as one of their essential functions, and in labelling their difficulties in providing it as a "major problem".

Although such an apparently straightforward matter, transport does lay bare a fundamental dilemma for Good Neighbour Schemes in their efforts to match care to need. The need for transport is, typically, a need for regular (and therefore expensive) support, often at inconvenient times – those that suit the professional services rather than the volunteers or the clients – and sometimes involving long (and therefore very expensive) journeys. A genuine neighbourly relationship could sustain such a service uncomplainingly, as part of a long-standing pattern of reciprocal concern. But where no such taken-for-granted basis of involvement already exists, the question of costs must be faced. If helpers refuse to meet the costs themselves, the scheme wilts or collapses. If they do meet the costs, the attempt to encourage neighbourliness is in danger of being perverted either by an undue emphasis on service delivery or by no less biased ideas of "good works". Because neighbourliness is above all a matter of reciprocity, the problem of providing transport unerringly reveals the tension between the two aims of Good Neighbour Schemes; it makes an urgent practical issue out of a general problem.

Before concluding this discussion of problems, we should like to stress once again – since it was so insistently stressed by our informants – the extent to which the supply of Good Neighbours is seen to be affected by the increasing tendency for women to have full-time jobs, a tendency that was in turn related to the poor state of the national economy. In other words, here is further evidence that *Good Neighbour Schemes are a phenomenon of affluence.* Or, perhaps more fairly and adequately, one should say the evidence suggests that, as a form of social care, *Good Neighbour Schemes can be expected to flourish naturally only against the background of certain kinds and levels of economic prosperity and security.* As that background is withdrawn, Good Neighbouring seems increasingly to need organised public support.

*The relationship between schemes and external welfare agencies, both statutory and voluntary,* and *the internal organisation and administration of schemes* were both reported as "major problems" by almost one in five of our informants. These two broad categories, however, mask a multitude of different problems. As a result, generalised statistics are not very helpful in this context. For example, the problem of "organisation and administration" actually involves matters as diverse as: the difficulty of finding people to fill positions of responsibility; maintaining effective communication among all those involved in a scheme; organising work rotas for helpers or filing systems on clients; personality clashes between organisers; finding premises; working out reliable methods for discovering need without being intrusive; processing referrals; maintaining the morale of helpers; matching helpers to clients – and, in addition to all this, trying to minimise internal bureaucracy!

The problem of the relationship between schemes and other agencies – above all, the statutory authorities – is not quite so various in its forms, but it does include complaints about: too little contact with the Social Services, and too much contact; the reluctance of some authorities to give schemes information they need in order to help their clients, and the "dumping" on schemes of difficult cases that social workers want to get rid of.

In broad terms, both types of problem seem to be spread fairly evenly among all types of scheme and throughout all regions of the country. However, schemes initiated by the churches are a good deal more likely than others to feel that they lack adequate contact with the Social Services, and schemes in the North and in Yorkshire and Humberside are twice as likely as those elsewhere to conclude that they would be more successful if they had more contact with statutory agencies. Conversely, schemes in the South East are more likely than those elsewhere to suffer from (or to report that they suffer from) internal administrative problems.

But to go beyond such general patterns and really to discover what these problems mean for Good Neighbour Schemes, it is necessary to abandon statistics and turn to individual cases. For the purposes of this discussion we have concentrated on the schemes reported to us from the counties of Hampshire and West Sussex, and have tried to describe the incidence and manifestations of just two problems: relations with the statutory services, and internal central administration.

Hampshire and West Sussex are, of course, among the counties best supplied with Good Neighbour Schemes (although their neighbour, Surrey, seems to have the highest incidence of schemes, both absolutely and relative to population, of any English county). Yet there are important differences between the two counties. One of those differences is *the extent to which the relationship between Good Neighbour Schemes and external welfare agencies is shaped by the external agencies themselves.*

Thus, at the time of our survey, the Church of England and the County Social Services Department in Hampshire had collaborated to appoint a Community Care Groups Adviser, who seems to have interpreted community care as involving, among other things, active support for Good Neighbouring. We discovered the existence and importance of the Adviser indirectly, as informant after informant from all parts of the county told us of the part she had played in initiating and supporting their schemes. In fact, she was in touch with 59 schemes throughout Hampshire and had evidently been a source of much positive help for many of them. At least as important as her personal enthusiasm, however, was the fact that she represented a practical expression of County Council support for Good Neighbour Schemes.

Hampshire, in fact, was one of the few county authorities that had a coherent policy of encouraging Good Neighbouring. Even before local government reorganisation in 1974 the Portsmouth authority had been appointing Good Neighbour Organisers, and by 1977 the county authority as a whole seems to have had a clear picture of a system of complementary community care services in which Good Neighbour Schemes played an integral part alongside community workers, community care groups and a host of more specialised services. The Social Services Department was actively involved (often in conjunction with the churches, but also in direct response to requests from local residents) in providing advice and help in "the setting up and servicing of new groups. . . very much as a joint venture". Compared with the national average of 38 per cent, we found that just over 70 per cent of schemes in Hampshire received grants from the Social Services; admittedly quite small ones – the average was £24 – but they established a positive relationship. We think that this must have had something to do with the fact that *not one* of the Hampshire schemes reported to us listed relations with the statutory authorities among their major problems.

West Sussex, although similar to Hampshire in most demographic respects and in the incidence of Good Neighbour Schemes in relation to population, presented a strikingly different picture. Here there was no discernible County Council policy towards Good Neighbouring. There had been a patchy response at divisional and district level to the "Be a Good Neighbour" campaign. In one or two places the resources of the Job Creation Programme had been used to sustain a network of schemes – although we were told that it was not clear whether this support would survive once the subsidised posts came to an end. Elsewhere in the county, most Social Services Area Offices said that they had no plans for Good Neighbour Schemes and little or no knowledge of any schemes operating in their territory (even though we discovered that quite a number were in fact operating). In the town of Crawley, where schemes seemed to be particularly numerous, we learned that many of them owed their origins to one particular Community Worker who left the area in 1975. Since then, as one of the organisers put it, "help from the Social Services has been intermittent – no finance and little liaison". Compared with the national average of 38 per cent, only 30 per cent of West Sussex schemes reported to us receive grants from statutory sources.

This evidence of official indifference to Good Neighbour Schemes should not be taken to suggest that West Sussex County Council is in fact failing to ensure that the kinds of care and help characteristically provided by Good Neighbour Schemes are also provided in West Sussex. This authority seems rather to have found other ways of doing things; in particular, the visiting services organised by some of the older-established voluntary organisations and by the Councils for Voluntary Service are quite heavily relied upon.

Still, a lack of official enthusiasm for Good Neighbour Schemes is certainly reflected in the way schemes in West Sussex view their problems. One in three of the schemes reported to us from that county included among their problems their relationship with the statutory services. Almost without exception the complaints were of a simple lack of contact. Sometimes there was difficulty in obtaining information about available services, and sometimes social workers failed to provide adequate background information about cases referred to the schemes, or failed to refer at all. Most fundamental was the awareness of the apparent absence of anyone "up there" who was in any way interested in what schemes were trying to do: "if only we could have a Community Worker like Mrs. Godfrey again"; "you'd think they could spare someone to come and give a talk now and then". A more useful, and perhaps more realistic, assessment of the problem was, however, made by one organiser who suggested that the Good Neighbours were ignored because "what with the Social Services and the WRVS, there's really not much left for us to do". The scheme depended upon existing agencies to give it work – but, quite possibly, those agencies were doing the work perfectly well already. In such circumstances, presumably, an authority would have to be convinced of the special merits of encouraging neighbourliness *over and above* providing social care before it could be persuaded to support the special type of care represented by Good Neighbouring.

To return now to the national picture, we can see that Hampshire and West Sussex are extreme examples of a range of possible *relationships between schemes and the statutory authorities which, taken as a whole, can be said to be characterised by ambiguity and contingency rather than by either positive support or positive hostility and neglect.* Any given authority will be operating a complex system of social care services in collaboration with a more or less extensive array of voluntary organisations, and somewhere within the system there will be someone with at least a watching brief for Good Neighbour Schemes. For their part, schemes are set up – often quite consciously, as many of our informants made clear – with a view to closing some kind of gap in the existing welfare system. The gap may be perceived as a matter of "emergency services", or of drawing isolated people into the web of social care through various kinds of contacts, street-wardens or visiting networks – schemes seem fairly evenly divided between the two views.

But in either case the business of filling the gap does involve the making of contacts not only between local residents but also between the schemes and the established welfare agencies. It is here that the ambiguity and contingency pervading the relationship between schemes and the statutory authorities are likely to make life difficult for Good Neighbours.

A few organisers of schemes, and a few Social Services Department officials, seem happy to envisage the kind of relationship in which schemes end up as little more than an adjunct of the welfare state. Conversely, a few organisers of schemes are anxious to maintain complete independence from the statutory agencies, seeing neighbourliness as essentially an alternative to the welfare state, or at least as something that can only develop beyond the reach of bureaucracy; about 2 per cent of the "major problems" reported to us involved a desire to make more room for Good Neighbouring by restricting statutory activity.

But for the vast majority both of organisers and social service officials, *the issue seems to be to work out a relationship that permits schemes both to 'fill the gap' and to enjoy relative independence.* Not surprisingly, those schemes initiated directly by statutory bodies or officials were most likely to be satisfied with their present relationship with the statutory agencies. Among the others, however, there was often a marked ambivalence: "they were supposed to give us back-up support, but after we became critical of social workers' lack of action in a number of cases their support was gradually withdrawn"; "first of all they tried to run the scheme completely, now they don't want to know about us", or conversely, "when we first began they refused to take any interest, treated us as meddling amateurs really; now that the day centre is such a success they want to run the whole show".

From the point of view of most organisers and members of schemes, the problem is to secure the support they need to function efficiently without interference – to have liaison without being pressed to reduce the *ad hoc* and necessarily untidy informality of Good Neighbouring to the accountable order of a social service. In fact, very few (if any) Social Services Departments seem to have any kind of policy about co-operation at area or district level with Good Neighbour Schemes. Where Good Neighbour volunteers are used by social workers, or where cases are referred by social workers to the organisers of schemes, this appears in all cases – as the examples of Hampshire and West Sussex suggest – to be a result of decisions on the part of individual social workers. The schemes that work closely with social workers do so because the individual social workers concerned have recognised their value. In the absence of policy, working relationships are naturally very variable: "We used to have very good liaison with the local authority but rapid turnover of social workers has meant that we've lost contact – the new social workers don't really know us"; "We need to find ways of making better links between the scheme and social workers and hospitals so that the family is cared for and information exchanged much more smoothly".

To sum up, on the one hand "it is essential that open communication and contact be encouraged" between the social services and the schemes, and ideally that there should be a regular flow of referrals, in which social workers really trust Good Neighbours to provide care without supervision; on the other hand, there needs to be a "general recognition by the statutory services that there are 'caring groups' such as ours which do not have a

48

formal framework, but which *will* use natural local care". Again, the problem is seen as one of *respecting the boundaries* between the formal and informal sectors. They should be linked, but neither should be allowed to incorporate the other: "The scheme must be a really local, friendly scheme if it is to work, but it needs unobtrusive liaison between the SSD, NHS, Volunteer Bureau and the local people too"; "To really do our job we need a much better flow of information both ways between ourselves and the statutory services". Not control, but dialogue; above all, information about where care is needed and how it can be obtained.

This majority *emphasis on dialogue without control* is important in view of the fact that a rather different minority view seems to be developing within some statutory agencies. Thus, in one county where Good Neighbour Schemes have been linked to the Home Help Service, we were told (by the social worker responsible) that "consideration might well have to be given to clearer policies within County Councils regarding conditions, recommended pay and provisions and in general conditions of services for Good Neighbours". Some formulation of policy does seem to be widely desired, and is certainly desirable; but the overwhelming opinion within the schemes themselves is plainly *against* this policy of administrative incorporation and rationalisation and *in favour of* dialogue. We feel that this is a correct view of what is needed if the ideal of neighbouring, as understood by the schemes, is to have any substantive reality.

The trouble is that, although Good Neighbour Schemes rightly understand that, in order to realise their special objectives, they must be seen as distinct from – and must in principle differ from – organised social welfare, they are at the same time aware that, in certain practical respects, *organised welfare holds the keys to their own survival.* Those keys are information, cases and, above all (or so our respondents seem to think), cash: "Our only complaint really is that we can't get a small grant to relieve the constant pressure of worrying about whether we can afford to keep going"; "Our scheme costs very little to operate in its present limited form but cannot be extended until such time as we can afford staff to man the office"; "If more money were available we could go further afield with the scheme; after all, we have one of the largest populations of elderly people in the country"; "More money is our main problem; we are not able to subsidise many activities because we are self-supporting and therefore short of money". Despite the frequency of such statements, however, we are not convinced that a guaranteed income from external sources would really enable more schemes to develop patterns of care that significantly resemble neighbourly relationships. But we *are* convinced that many organisers and members of schemes interpret their failure to develop such patterns in financial terms, and that *a few experiments in subsidising Good Neighbouring in a relatively generous way would therefore be worthwhile* as a means of determining just how significant lack of finance really is. *Prima facie,* it seems that money to spend on publicity,

49

on administrative help, or on a newsletter or a minibus, would help to establish the presence and viability of a Good Neighbour Scheme within its locality. Whether more publicity, more administrative assistance and better transport would also help to bring together provision of care and the cultivation of neighbourliness is a moot point. But it could quite easily be tested experimentally.

The problems of *internal organisation and administration* that schemes face are rather different and highly varied. Interestingly, however, most of them seem to reflect the basic dilemmas of matching care to need and of reconciling help with neighbourliness that we have found underlying the "major problems" discussed above. Furthermore, the most frequently-suggested solution to problems of internal organisation – the appointment of a full-time paid organiser – would call for a significant increase in outside financial support. In this respect, our two sample counties of Hampshire and West Sussex reflect the general pattern well: 20 per cent of schemes in Hampshire and 18 per cent of schemes in West Sussex reported major problems of organisation and administration. Despite their differences in detail, perhaps the most striking feature of these problems is the way they confirm the impression that a *large proportion of schemes depend for their existence and success upon the drive, commitment and co-ordinating skills of a single individual.* Often the "problem" of administration turns out to consist of this central person trying unsuccessfully to devolve responsibilities on to a committee. Or the committee is anxiously trying to find a replacement for a central person who has moved away: "Our main problem is simply to find someone to take over from Mrs Hibbert and organise the scheme". Or it is a matter of finding an income for an existing central person so that her or his energies can be devoted even more fully to the scheme. Sometimes it is even a matter of reorganising the entire operation of a scheme so that an individual rather than a committee can take charge effectively: "Originally the scheme was run by one person. It grew too much work for one so a committee was formed. Then the area was divided geographically into three with a co-ordinator for each area. Our biggest problem is finding the *right* person to be co-ordinator". The right person seems to be someone who can not only handle the complex and taxing work of co-ordinating helpers and those in need of help, but can also keep sight of the fact that Good Neighbour Schemes are ultimately about the promotion of neighbourliness – and therefore that being the key figure in a scheme means, paradoxically, constantly working to make it less centralised and more representative and participatory, and above all not to expect much personal prominence and glory. It is remarkable how many such people there seem to be.

Crucial as the central individual often is, Good Neighbour Schemes are basically about community involvement. Many of their problems of administration and organisation therefore seem to *reflect the unavoidable tension between an inward-looking, centralising tendency towards efficient service-management and the outward-looking, decentralising logic of the Good Neighbour.* Once again, the balance must be struck between getting things done and getting people involved. Many schemes seem, in practice, to see-saw uneasily between these two aims: "We find that a smaller group, as we now are, is easier to run, but it could become cliqueish"; "We try to keep all 50 of our 'street contacts' involved in the running of the scheme – but that's a full time job in itself. I find I have less and less time to do anything else"; "When we started we planned to make all decisions at a general meeting of everyone interested but unfortunately it didn't work out – after two or three bad rows about priorities we switched to a small committee with one representative from each group of streets"; and, as a last resort, "Personally I have got bogged-down with regular visits to elderly housebound people and haven't time to recruit new helpers – I have asked the WRVS to take over the organisation". But perhaps the most ironic – and perceptive – comment on this dilemma came from an organiser in a large Hampshire village, who wrote: "We all agree that a scheme like ours should be informal and unobtrusive – but at present the scheme is fading because hardly anyone seems to know we exist". That is getting very close to a Good Neighbour Scheme version of *Catch 22*!

The last "major problem" that we feel demands attention at this stage seems at first sight quite different from those we have discussed so far: *having too few people to help.* Here, the national average of 15 per cent is misleading; there are major regional variations and, perhaps more pertinently, quite dramatic variations between town and country. For example, almost 30 per cent of the schemes in West Sussex and Hampshire that admitted to "major problems" complained of a dearth of clients – and all of them were in rural areas. But only one of the West Yorkshire schemes reported to us and only two in London (2 per cent in each case) suffered from this problem.

All Good Neighbour Schemes have a problem in finding clients, in publicising their existence and in convincing their prospective public of their ability to provide help. But that is rather different from the sense of possible irrelevance or redundancy that seems to have led some of our informants to identify a shortage of clients as their major problem. Oddly enough, it was often suggested that the root of the problem lay in the fact that there is either too much natural neighbourliness or too little need for social care in a particular neighbourhood to sustain a Good Neighbour Scheme – despite the willingness of many residents to join such a scheme as helpers. Again and again our informants told us of magnificent starts: "Street links were made in every street in the neighbourhood"; "Over 100 people volunteered in the first month" – only to go on to describe a dreadful withering-away as the volunteers found they had nothing to do: "The street links became frustrated and apathetic because residents wouldn't use them"; "They lost enthusiasm and drifted away when they found the scheme was all helpers and hardly anyone to help".

51

The general tenor of such complaints is quite clear: "People seem reluctant to use us". But, beyond that, there are in fact two separate issues: *the problem of the neighbourhood where there is really no need for a Good Neighbour Scheme*, despite the enthusiasm of residents; and *the problem of the neighbourhood where the needs that a scheme could meet do exist, but where those in need cannot be induced to turn to a Good Neighbour Scheme for help.* The former is characteristically a problem of schemes in well-established rural villages; the latter of schemes in suburbs, town and new estates. The problem in the villages seems to be simply that there *are* no problems – in effect, our informants were describing communities where neighbourliness had already developed to such a pitch that almost all of the cases that a scheme might otherwise have handled were adequately dealt with by informal means. At best, an organisation would merely formalise what already operated informally. Thus: "This is a rural area and on the whole community care is good, so the need is not as great as in the cities"; "In a village such as this most people have good neighbours and can get lifts and help when required – the most we can do is provide a long-stop"; "The level of spontaneous caring activities in our neighbourhood seems to be very high and we hear of many cases where a rota of people is organised quite informally to sit up at night with a dying relative, look after children if the mother is ill and so on"; "I'm always coming across individuals who are helping other individuals in our neighbourhood without any connection with the care group, so maybe we don't need an organisation".

In fact, this "problem" of an absence of need is more common than is implied by its 15 per cent incidence among "major problems" reported to us. About one in five of the 42 per cent of schemes that said they had no major problems went on to describe their "success" in terms of an apparent lack of need for their services – a consequence of the fact that they happened to be operating in a community which had strong natural neighbouring networks anyway: "Most people here are mainly cared for by their immediate neighbours"; "We're just a co-ordinating body in this friendly community"; "Most people in this village have good neighbours – there's constant visiting"; "Most of the things we do people here would do anyway".

The difference between those informants who saw such a state of affairs as a "major problem" and those who saw it as a "success" was often that the former were not quite convinced that *all* the social need in their friendly communities was being met by natural neighbourliness. Rather, they seem to have found that, while there was a shortage of clients in the sense that almost all the services that Good Neighbour Schemes could most appropriately provide were being provided informally, an actual or potential residuum of need existed which informal neighbouring might ignore because it was too difficult to be handled informally and which a scheme, lacking a broad community basis, could not easily meet either. *The general shortage of clients leads to a shortage of helpers and resources, which in turn means that even the few clients there are cannot be cared for effectively.* Thus: "Most people are well looked after by their neighbours here, and that leaves the isolated type of individual, for example psychiatric cases, to be dealt with by us – and most of our helpers, being untrained, are not really willing or able to take on that kind of work"; "Even in a very friendly place like this there are some people living in remote cottages or people without friends or relatives; but with so little for our volunteers to do on a day-to-day basis we haven't been able to develop the contacts or the transport arrangements they might need"; or, more bitterly: "This is a small village and most people here are well cared-for or able to look after themselves; they seem to take the view that it's just too bad on those few who are less fortunate than themselves". Somewhere in even the most neighbourly communities there are small pockets of need that these informants cannot bring themselves to ignore, but which are too small to sustain a full-blown Good Neighbour Scheme.

The other aspect of the problem of a shortage of clients is quite different. Most of the people who mentioned it to us saw it as a problem of trust. Many local residents are known to be in need of the kinds of social care that Good Neighbour Schemes can provide, but *the bridge from need to neighbourliness by way of care doesn't get built;* either because those residents are unaware that a local scheme exists, or because they are adequately looked after by other, statutory or voluntary agencies, or – most commonly, in the judgement of our informants – because "they don't seem to trust us". The solution to the first of these difficulties is usually, and sensibly, seen to be more publicity; or perhaps more *appropriate* publicity – one organiser told us that her committee had just decided to attempt a house-to-house newsletter after an unsuccessful campaign based largely on posters displayed in banks! The solution to the second is more complicated: according to the extent to which schemes are committed to encouraging neighbourliness as well as to meeting needs, they must negotiate some space for themselves with the existing care-providing organisations.

Here again, the policies of those organisations is a decisive factor. Several informants told us that they had in fact been quite successful in persuading a statutory or voluntary agency (a Community Development Officer, say, or a local branch of Age Concern) to make room for a scheme and to work constructively with it within an existing pattern of care and service. As the policy statements we have collected in chapter 5 suggest, many of the agencies in question do have very positive attitudes towards the encouragement of neighbourliness as an end in itself, and these are presumably reflected in the many local arrangements between schemes and various welfare organisations. In a few cases, however, the attempt to negotiate some space for Good Neighbouring had obviously failed. The existing service providers – in these cases usually statutory bodies – had apparently failed to see the value of Good Neighbouring as a complement to what they themselves were doing. The third aspect of the problem, the unwillingness of potential clients to trust a scheme, is much the hardest to solve and the most damaging to the morale of helpers and organisers: "It's very difficult to go on offering help when you feel people just don't want it".

The problem of *persuading residents to trust Good Neighbour Schemes* was outlined to us in several different ways. Schemes found that many of the people that they – or a social worker, doctor or community nurse – considered to be in need were simply unwilling to admit their need to other local people: "It's a matter of pride"; "You know they could do with the help but they don't like to ask for it"; "Some people don't mind getting help from their families but they won't ask anything from outsiders". Beyond that, there seems to be a more general barrier of mistrust: "Many people have never heard of us, others get confused and think we are paid social workers and some think we are home helps; the elderly cannot always understand what we are trying to do – they are taught to be cautious and often we aren't even admitted to their homes as a result; our helpers carry identity cards but this often just adds to the confusion"; "Statutory services are using us more and more but there is surprisingly little demand for some of our activities, particularly sitting-in . . . we feel that under-use of this section is to do with the personal involvement required and the necessary trust and confidence which it entails".

Over and above calls for more and better publicity, and calls for other organisations, both statutory and voluntary, to make room for schemes, this awareness of the *need to build trust as a condition for Good Neighbouring* is a constant – and, in our view, highly perceptive – theme of the replies to our survey. It draws attention to a fundamental problem in the linking of care to need within a setting of local neighbourliness. The need may be there and the readiness to help may be there. Problems of logistics and publicity can be solved. But, beyond all that, people still need to be convinced that "they can trust us to help and not to interfere". That kind of trust is, of course, the very basis upon which 'natural' neighbourly care and help flourish. Very few of our informants who had identified this basic problem for organised Good Neighbouring could suggest ways of solving it. In new, dispersed or socially mixed neighbourhoods it was felt to be particularly intractable. The third and fifth case studies in the next chapter illustrate the problem in greater detail and also perhaps suggest some practical ways in which it can be overcome.

## Success

In all this, we must not forget that 24 per cent of our informants said their schemes had experienced no "major problems", and 29 per cent could not even think of ways in which their schemes could be more successful. There is no doubt that many schemes in all parts of the country are thought to be working very well. Moreover, this feeling of success seems to reflect, in many cases, a genuine achievement in terms of *both* the basic aims of Good Neighbour Schemes; that is, schemes have managed to provide forms of help and care not provided in their neighbourhoods by other agencies and in so doing have built up a stronger sense of neighbourliness and mutal involvement among significant numbers of local people.

The statistical presentation of the functions and problems of schemes that we have used so far tends to obscure the number and variety of the types of success that were also reported to us. Only when we cross-checked the information obtained through our questionnaire to organisers by interviewing clients and residents in selected neighbourhoods did the achievements of many schemes become clear. Organisers do not usually boast about, or even describe, the successes of their schemes. That part of the picture is best obtained from clients and residents – those who are most keenly aware of how a scheme can change the quality of life. The comments of one client we interviewed must speak for the majority: "About a year after we moved here my husband went into hospital and was given three months to live. I had joined our scheme as a helper and hadn't expected to be one of the helped. But every day throughout that three months someone from the scheme drove me to the hospital, waited for me and drove me home. And it wasn't just driving. More often than not I'd been invited to their homes for a cup of tea or a chat. We were strangers here and I was terrified of being left on my own. The way it worked out, I've got more friends here now than I've ever had. I can't think how I'd have managed that time without them".

But before we begin to describe how successful Good Neighbour Schemes work, we must note two respects in which a sense of "success" can be misleading. Firstly, as already pointed out, what some schemes see as success is interpreted by others as a shortage of clients, and hence a problem. In other words: "There were many good neighbours in this village already so it wasn't very difficult to launch the scheme – all we had to do was to link up what was already there to the Social Services". *Many schemes embody and express an existing high level of neighbourliness and so have few problems in promoting it.* Secondly, the apparent success of many schemes is quite clearly related to the fact that they have deliberately restricted their activities to those things they can do well: "We are successful because we have limited our aims – the main thing we do is take people to hospital"; "We are an emergency service only – we haven't the means to develop long-term care"; "We don't attempt to deal with long-term care and attention – such cases have to be referred to the appropriate agency"; "We see our task as co-ordinating the activities of others rather than providing new services ourselves". *There is a more or less deliberate restriction of the aims of a scheme* to those activities that are immediately useful and are feasible within the available framework of resources and contacts. Realistic though this may be, it does imply that the broader aim of promoting general neighbourliness has been abandoned; the scheme has retreated from the goals implicit in our definition of Good Neighbouring to a more conventional pattern of

55

voluntary service. Such a shift of emphasis is significant, since so many of our informants insisted that the whole point about Good Neighbour Schemes was that "we are not a voluntary service or a group of do-gooders" but something more deeply-rooted in the community. It is in terms of that ideal that the success of schemes must be assessed.

Fortunately, the information we received does allow us at least to begin such an assessment. Somewhat to our surprise, a quite clear sense of what constitutes success did emerge from the answers to our questionnaire, together with a rather more tentative sense of how that success might be achieved. For both Good Neighbour Schemes and conventional voluntary service projects, an obvious measure of success would be a substantial decrease in unmet need in the area where the scheme or project operates. But whereas for the conventional voluntary service project, as for the statutory social services, such a success would certainly be connected with the presence of some smoothly-functioning formal organisation, for a genuine Good Neighbour Scheme the elimination of need would be directly linked with the elimination of formal caring organisations (including Good Neighbour Schemes) as well. "We'd like to think we were unnecessary", as one organiser put it; "For us, success would be if there was no-one in the town who needed our help"; "We'll have succeeded when everything we do is done on an informal basis by local people themselves".

*The Good Neighbour Scheme, in other words, is a Cheshire Cat among organisations:* ideally, having boldly appeared on the local scene, it would eventually disappear gracefully into the informal fabric of community life, leaving only neighbourliness behind it. Success for such projects should be assessed in terms of how far the formal provision of care has indeed been absorbed into the everyday practice of neighbourly relationships. Or as one secretary put it more realistically: "If our street contact system really got going only very loose background co-ordination would be necessary – the scheme would work on its own".

In practice, of course, most schemes are too involved in meeting specific needs, too concerned with the immediate problems of matching help to need, too conscious of the difficulties of merging their work into the informal networks of local life and, above all perhaps, too sharply aware of the need to win recognition as appropriate and reliable helpers both from those in need and from other caring agencies, to expect to be able to "disappear gracefully" at an early date. What schemes do seem to envisage, however, is a state of affairs in which Good Neighbouring might gradually, and in a piecemeal fashion, enlarge the role of the good neighbour, shifting the balance of social care so that informal care between local residents becomes a little more effective and widespread and formal social care by professional and voluntary organisations a little less all-pervading and indispensable.

From the comments of our informants we were able to construct a picture of something like *an ideal Good Neighbour Scheme*. It would cover a small area,

56

probably no more than 2000 households. Each street would have its own Good Neighbour or Street Contact, who would be fully informed of the needs of other residents in the area and be accepted as the kind of person to whom others naturally turned for advice and help. These key helpers would also be sufficiently 'trained' in the ways of the health and welfare services and of other sources of care to be able, when asked, to make contacts or give advice quickly and precisely. The scheme would thus be highly localised and require loose co-ordination but little formal organisation. The Good Neighbours themselves would, however, be a mixture of skills and types – male and female, young and old. The organiser or co-ordinator would be paid – even if only part-time – and one member, either the co-ordinator or someone else (possibly themselves disabled or housebound), would be available at all times to receive messages and to pass on problems that the Good Neighbours could not themselves handle. To make possible this rapid contact and response, telephones would be supplied to those Good Neighbours who did not already have them. Social Services offices would make referrals and be ready to offer advice, but would not interfere in the running of the scheme. Doctors and other relevant professional people in the area would play a similar supportive role. The Good Neighbours would meet regularly with one another and the organiser, and perhaps with social workers, doctors, clergymen and others with whom the work and problems of the scheme could be discussed. The meetings would be important for the morale of the scheme, since they would allow professionals to show their appreciation and members to "pat each other on the back". Expenses would be made available to meet necessary transport costs (wherever these could not be recouped from clients) and also perhaps to ensure some publicity for the scheme (a postcard in every home and occasional circulars are the favoured methods). Helpers would be properly insured against accidents. For the rest, the emphasis would be on supporting and gradually extending natural neighbouring networks and stressing the value of informal as against formal caring. Thus, in addition to providing help themselves, members would try to bring together residents who might be able to help each other. Over and above any specific giving of care, the scheme would have a fairly intense social life. *Gradually, distinctions between helpers and clients would disappear.*

Of course, only a tiny minority of schemes – mostly in compact, isolated areas – even begin to approximate to this ideal. A perhaps more viable "second best" is also discernible in the comments of our respondents. In view of the fact that many schemes will have to be responsible for much larger areas, and that close proximity of Good Neighbours and residents will therefore not be immediately possible, the organisation will need to be slightly more centralised. In these circumstances, good telephone links between the organiser and each Good Neighbour will be even more necessary, to ensure as much dispersal and localisation of the work as possible.

Good transport facilities (often specified as a minibus) will be equally vital, to enable the organiser to match appropriate Good Neighbours to the problems that arise. Once again, the health and welfare professionals are seen as having a positive, but very much a *background*, relationship to the scheme, as sources of referrals, information and "recognition" – but in no sense as managers or controllers. A distinctive feature of this "second-best" scheme is the widely-perceived need for a building that will serve as a meeting-place and Day Centre, where isolated people, not otherwise in touch with the scheme or with any easily-identified social network, can come together and meet others, and where a wider variety of local residents can mix and perhaps build up relationships. Most importantly, funds would be made available to permit payment of expenses – on however modest a scale – to helpers, thus ensuring the recruitement and retention of helpers in "difficult" areas where volunteers could not otherwise be found.

In so far as Good Neighbour Schemes are pursuing distinct social purposes of their own and are not succumbing to the temptation to become simply an ancillary arm of the welfare state, these are the ideal conditions that they hope to achieve. Whether such schemes could really succeed in constructing effective and inclusive networks of informal social care is obviously a matter for continuing practical experiment.

In sum, the major problem facing Good Neighbour Schemes is how to match the helping resources available locally to the neighbourhood's actual needs, and how to do so with as much informality and as little bureaucracy as possible. This general problem raises more specific issues about the supply of helpers, the co-ordination of their efforts, relations with other agencies, contact with those in need and the availability of finance. Even more specifically, there are worries about publicity, telephones and trans-port, about the attitudes of particular social workers, doctors, nurses and ministers of religion, about insurance and expenses, about suitable internal adminstrative arrangements, and about the replacement of heroic central individuals who have moved away or retired. At the time of our survey, however, it seemed that, on balance, the prevailing mood among Good Neighbour Schemes was one of quiet confidence that, given time, most of these problems could be overcome.

# IV
# Cases and Contexts

In this chapter we shall turn aside from the general findings of our survey in order to examine in detail some particular examples of Good Neighbour Schemes. The schemes chosen are not necessarily representative of schemes as a whole, but we feel that they do illustrate usefully – and sometimes dramatically – both the achievements and the dilemmas of organised Good Neighbouring. In earlier chapters we stressed how much the prospects of Good Neighbour Schemes are affected by the existing pattern of social care in their areas. To develop this point, one of the case studies in this chapter concerns a whole city and another a complete London borough; both illustrate how existing statutory and voluntary agencies can 'make room' for Good Neighbouring within an established pattern of care and service. We could also have given many examples of cities, boroughs or counties where the statutory and voluntary authorities have concluded that they are managing to provide caring services perfectly well already, and so have more or less deliberately *not* made room for Good Neighbour Schemes. We also wish to develop the point made earlier about the crucial nature of the problem, faced by almost all Good Neighbour Schemes, of matching help to need; two of the case studies below are intended to show that, in practical terms, this problem is difficult to solve but absolutely fundamental to the promotion of Good Neighbouring. Finally, we have chosen two schemes considered by those involved in them to have been a success, although in rather different ways; in both cases, the awareness of success seems to us to be closely related to the fact that the schemes started out with clear objectives which they made a determined *organisational* effort to realise. We wished to underline the paradox that, although Good Neighbouring is primarily concerned with the encouragement of informal caring relationships, if it is to succeed it must be based on carefully thought-out formal arrangements and strategies. But we will let the examples speak for themselves.

## 1 Pitside, County Durham
Pitside is a small town in County Durham with one of the oldest coal-mines in the region. Until thirty years ago it was a flourishing mining community boasting, among other things, two theatres, two golf-courses and a host of active sporting and social clubs and institutions. Along with most communities of its type, it suffered drastically from the contraction of the

North-East coalfield and, although it is among the towns scheduled for development by the county planning authorities, the remnants of its mining past are still more evident than the beginnings of its diversified light industrial future.

Pitside has, however, been a favoured target of social policy in County Durham. Alongside the many remaining terraces of pit houses, it has a good stock of modern council housing. Its old people are well catered-for in five different types of sheltered housing development. And it has a lively Good Neighbour Scheme launched by a Community Development Officer of the Social Services Department. The scheme had existed for almost three years at the time of our survey and had 40 registered Good Neighbours, excluding the variety of Councillors, clergymen and social workers associated with it in different organising or supportive capacities. Despite its official origins, it had no paid organiser and offered no financial rewards to its helpers. Our main interest in studying it was to find out who joins Good Neighbour Schemes and why.

Almost all the Good Neighbours were recruited through local churches – Roman Catholic, Church of England, Methodist and Salvation Army. The appeal to religious duty by vicars, priests and ministers was in most cases the initial spur to involvement – but it was seldom sufficient to sustain lasting participation. Many dropped out after a few weeks, excusing themselves in terms such as: "I was conned into it by Father Mulligan". Another striking feature of the scheme is the age distribution of the helpers: half are over 56, and only a third are under 40. The Pitside Good Neighbours are not bored young middle-class housewives, but mostly working-class people approaching or in the early years of retirement. And they share a strong sense of locality.

In addition to the watching brief of the Community Development Officer, the scheme has an exceptionally active local Councillor as its chairman ("she has always done everything in Pitside") and a dedicated voluntary secretary, who returned "home" at the age of 60 after running a hotel in Blackpool for several years and who described himself as "devoted to Pitside".

The basic activities of the scheme are home visiting and the running of day clubs at the Pitside Community Centre; there is a general meeting once a month to discuss the organisation, problems and policies of the scheme as a whole. Although the scheme appeared relatively stable in size and scope, both of its activities had in fact run into difficulties in the past. Attendance at the clubs, and the number of visits made, had both declined considerably since the launching of the scheme. On the visiting side, many of the original volunteers found either that they could not cope with the strain of knocking on doors and intruding themselves into other people's lives or that they were simply not needed – the streets assigned to them contained no-one who wanted their help or company. So far as the clubs were concerned, the

Pitside Scheme had gradually become almost exclusively concerned with care of the elderly; members who had joined hoping for other kinds of work steadily dropped out as this specialisation became clear: "I was very enthusiastic in the beginning...I persuaded lots of people to go to the meetings with me...I went to about half a dozen meetings and they went on and on about the elderly. I'm interested in the elderly, I can talk to them, but I didn't think it was going to be entirely for them". A day club for young mothers and their children had recently been launched to meet the evident demand for a Good Neighbour Scheme that would benefit people other than the elderly: "It's for depressed mums who are at home with small children". Despite this innovation, however, the Pitside Scheme was generally perceived as being a service for the elderly; its distinctive character lay in the fact that it was also seen to provide help *for* the elderly *by* the not-quite-so-elderly.

Each registered Good Neighbour in the scheme is assigned responsibility for a street, either the one in which she or he lives or one nearby. Although it did mobilise the existing resources of neighbourly relationships, this allocation also resulted in many Good Neighbours concluding that their help was not needed: "I did myself out of a job – there aren't any people who are 'at risk' in my street; I knocked on every door – and I hate knocking on doors – but there aren't any". There was a similar feeling of redundancy among many of the Good Neighbours whose main activity was helping at day clubs; "It's ridiculous sometimes – there are more helpers than handi-capped"; "Eight Good Neighbours and four old people – it doesn't make sense"; "The trouble is, there's more chiefs than Indians in this scheme". Yet old people still do fall ill, die or suffer acute loneliness without contact in Pitside. The scheme clearly had a logistics problem; it had not yet found the optimum way of mobilising the energies of its potential membership. Indeed, some residents felt that it had been quite indifferent to the problem of how to use the goodwill available. One keenly-felt instance was the decision of the organisers to change the time of the monthly meetings from evening to afternoon. Convenient as it was for the organisers, this change made participation in the scheme impossible for many of its original members and caused conflict of loyalties in many others. As a result, the scheme lost between a third and a half of its original members. This episode illustrates well the necessity for Good Neighbouring to balance the costs to helpers against the needs of the helped, and the ease with which the cost factor can be over-looked. Although several people had dropped out of the scheme, our conclusion is that they did so not because of a lack of goodwill or commitment, but because the organisers of the scheme had been unable to find ways of enabling them to realise their aims. The problem is one of how to organise the giving of help so that it fits conveniently into the lives of people who really wish to help but who also have other serious commitments.

We asked the Pitside Good Neighbours what they thought the scheme

61

was doing. Their answers revealed three distinct points of view. One-third of the Good Neighbours told us that their day clubs were the essential activity of the scheme; another third said that home visiting was its crucial role; almost all the remaining third said that they did not think that the scheme was doing anything of particular value, and many added that they were thinking of leaving it. The distribution of answers was closely related to underlying feelings about the ways in which help could and should be given. Thus, those who emphasised the importance of the day clubs also made clear their own unwillingness or inability to engage in home visiting; they stressed the value of the clubs because, for them, they were a safe and acceptable way of giving help, whereas home visiting was frightening and vaguely improper. In effect, the clubs *legitimised* involvement in the lives of strangers. Cooking meals at the Monday Club was unquestionably "helpful", yet did not presume a personal involvement with those who ate the meals. Here we have a category of Good Neighbours whose neighbour-liness is inhibited by an unwillingness to force themselves on those who need help. Being a helper at the club was a respectable way of making contact: "It gives you that bit of authority – otherwise I would never have known the old lady a few doors away". And through the clubs the slight diffidence about simply giving help was often offset by reciprocal advantages: "I go to the Monday Club every week. As well as going I get something out of it too – I get the company".

By contrast, those who emphasised the importance of visiting and helping people at home seemed to possess a *confidence* about their abilities as helpers that the Good Neighbours who concentrated on the clubs seemed to lack: "Of course I do a lot of visiting – I'm always popping in to see if someone is all right, or shopping if that is needed. But that's in me, I've always been like that. I've been secretary of the pensioners' club for thirty years and we do a lot for the old people. My mother ran the pensioners' club before me"; "All my life I've helped people – I never miss a day without going to see the old man who lives opposite". For some of these Good Neighbours, visiting seems to have become less a matter of helping and providing company than of offering a mixture of mothering and advocacy. These are the people who constantly lobby the organisers of the scheme and the Social Services Department for improvement in facilities: wheelchairs, a car to take the less mobile to the shops or the hairdresser, a visiting chiropodist, telephone links, more wardens in the sheltered housing. One of these groups had taken up the cause of an old woman who had not been allowed to join the Monday Club: "Well, she does smell a little but she can't get into a bath – the vicar told her she'd have to have a bath first if she wanted to go to the club". This case had become a major issue within the scheme and the Good Neighbour concerned was deeply embattled with the organisers: "I think they dread my talking now, but I shall go on – I'm that sort of person".

All the Good Neighbours in this group exhibited that kind of self-confidence. In most cases, it seemed to result from long experience of giving help in this particular locality; having spent all, or almost all, of their lives in Pitside, they could draw on a fund of knowledge about the community – and trust from its members – that broke down the barriers of reserve others found inhibiting. For many of them, indeed, "the scheme isn't doing anything very different from what I would normally do"; "I don't think you have to be connected to a scheme to be a good neighbour in a place like this; people help each other here". Experience of that kind is not, however, the only source of the confidence needed for active Good Neighbouring. Within this group there were others who stood out precisely because they were not old-established residents but newcomers. And considering that it is possible to live in Pitside for thirty years and still be thought – and feel – a stranger, these people's newness (a matter of less than four years) was clearly important for their involvement with the scheme. They wanted to join the community and the scheme was one way of doing it. The qualities they brought with them that enabled them to do more than just help at the day clubs was not simply a strong personality, but some relevant skill, training or experience: one had been a nurse, for example, and another an occupational therapist. Again, knowledge was the basis of their confidence in giving help, but in this case it was not knowledge of the network of people who needed help but of the specific ways in which that help could be given. They had *a trained ability to help*, both in the sense of knowing what to do and of wanting to be helpful; "I used to be a nurse and that made me more aware of helping people; I'm used to it and I miss it".

The third group of scheme members that we interviewed were all in various stages of withdrawing from it. They gave many reasons for their loss of commitment, but two in particular stood out: a feeling that the scheme was unnecessary – "you don't have to join an organisation to give a helping hand"; "we'd do it anyway" – and a sense of personal frustration within the scheme – "I'm thinking of stopping going, I feel so useless; I'm not in a position to lift any of the handicapped people...they've got more helpers than they need anyway"; "whenever you go there, it's the same people doing everything, they run it all"; "the ones who take all the glory never do the hard work"; or, simply, "there doesn't seem to be anyone for me to visit". Others, however, had not experienced these feelings, and had left simply because their involvement with the scheme had come to clash with other commitments, such as a new job or a sick relative. But the two main reasons for "dropping out" both seem to point to *structural* problems with the scheme. Feeling useless is not simply a consequence of the personality of the individual, but also of how a scheme employs its members: "I think it's ridiculous when you go to the Day Club and there's four handicapped people and eight helpers" is one aspect of that problem, and "I'd be happier if I could just do a bit – not have to do it every week" is another. The Pitside Scheme had been organised in terms of what the core group of organisers took to be the needs of their clients – but not in terms of the needs of its helpers. By contrast, the sense of the irrelevance of the scheme points to a quite different problem: how to demonstrate the *special* effectiveness of Good Neighbouring.

The scheme's activities were largely confined to what untrained, part-time amateurs could do to help others. Because the needs of the scheme's clients almost always went beyond those capabilities, it proved difficult to sustain conviction about the special value of the scheme. Members were constantly being reminded that the gap between the help they could give and the help their clients needed was one that had to be filled by specialists: "They could do with a nurse to help the people when they go to the toilets – not many of us can manage that"; "There really ought to be more full time wardens"; "They ought to vary the crafts at the Monday Club, but I'm no good at that sort of thing". Thus although two-thirds of the Pitside Good Neighbours saw their scheme as successful, it could clearly have been much more successful had it been able to solve two problems. One is essentially a question of internal organisation, of adjusting the scheme to the needs and capacities of the available helpers. But the other is an underlying scepticism about the value of organising the energies of ordinary people just because they *are* ordinary people. This feeling cuts both ways in Pitside; ordinary people would help others anyway, but the sort of help ordinary people can give is strictly limited. The scheme is a good thing but it is hard to see anything special about it.

But what struck us most in our interviews at Pitside was the widespread conviction that Good Neighbours should get something in return for the help they give. There was considerable diversity of opinion about what that return should be, but it was rare to find a Good Neighbour who would deny that there should be *some* kind of reciprocity. The only one who did recognised herself as a relic of a lost world: "I was brought up the old-fashioned way – give and don't expect anything in return. You don't find that now; everybody expects payment". As far as the Pitside Good Neighbours are concerned, she seems to be right. Whether or not some "do it for glory", as was widely believed, many others certainly do do it for the sake of simpler recognitions of their own needs. One of the questions we asked was "What sort of people are taking part in the scheme?" This produced three types of answer. First, there was frequent reference to the core group of organisers and long term residents who, it was said, "have always run Pitside"; "they've always helped all their lives"; "full of their own importance"; "some people have to be there – as an ornament, not for the work"; "domineering types"; "pushing themselves forward"; "genuinely trying to help people but it's got to be done their way". Secondly, and much more widespread, there was a sense of Good Neighbours as a whole being "just ordinary people", "people like me". This view was in turn linked to an awareness of the reciprocity implicit in Good Neighbouring: "They're much the same as me;

you're going to get old yourself one day and I'd like to think someone was going to visit me"; "Ordinary people – wanting to help each other"; "Nothing special about them; they get some kind of fulfilment, as I do"; and perhaps most concretely: "I've looked after an old lady of 76, but since I had the baby she's been more active than me; she's been doing things for me and bringing me bits of things; she comes in every day to see that I'm all right". Thirdly, there were those who felt, not surprisingly in a scheme recruited so predominantly through the churches, that the Good Neighbours were impelled by religious commitment. They give help "for God"; "If you've got any faith at all you should help people who are worse off".

Of these three views, the second was by far the most common. More than half the answers evoked the image of a community in which helpers and helped were linked by a shared "ordinariness", and thus by actual or potential reciprocity; a further third spoke of a dominant and "uncommon" minority motivated by self-importance; whilst the suggestion that people responded through religion to a norm of altruism was very much a minority view. Other answers and observations confirm this pattern. There is a small group of long term residents in Pitside who "do everything", who are aware of each other and themselves as doing everything, and who are constantly active on the public stage. These people see it as their responsibility to make things happen, and the return that they expect is confirmation from others that things are indeed happening. Their activism is not soley a matter of personality, however; in every relevant case at Pitside it was rooted in a life-time, and sometimes a family tradition, of giving help and being acknowledged as helpful. Our interviews with this group produced a set of autobiographies that dramatically document the creation of the relationship between helping and leadership within this small community. Here is a representative example:

> "I've organised trips for the old people for 12 years now...it was in my mother to be on Committees and I've followed on from her...I was on the Council for 18 years ...When I was young if anyone was dying the family or neighbours would always send for my mother to lay them out...when I was 25 I used to help her...there was one family of eight and six of them died within three years – I laid them all out...On a Sunday evening after chapel our doors were open to everyone...we had an organ and a piano, sometimes as many as 40 people would be in our house, you'd sit on the floor if the chairs were full... Nowadays it's all paid people doing things for the elderly ...some young woman comes here and she must be paid £30 a week and we've been doing it all these years for nothing ...they're paid for it out of our money and they're not

needed – we can do it and they're trying to edge us out… It's nice to know you've helped someone… I'm 68 and I've never been out of Pitside; my mother died last year at 94 and she'd never been out of Pitside either".

Most Good Neighbours are not motivated in this way. For them, the decisive consideration is the feasibility of an exchange of help between themselves and those they help. The notion of "ordinary people – wanting to help each other" rests on a simple expectation of reciprocity. Whether the return is made now – "I really value having someone to talk to; it does me as much good as it does her" – or in the future, there seems to be a fundamental belief that help can earn help. The negative aspect of this, of course, is a rather overt belief that help *should* earn help, that payment is due. One Good Neighbour, slightly disgruntled at not herself receiving help during a recent illness, said, with unconscious irony, that it would be better "if the helpers weren't quite so concerned in getting something out of it – it doesn't cost anything to go and see someone; Mrs B came to see me but she wanted me to look after her son in return". But, even though the balance of help is not always maintained with sensitivity or symmetry, we were left in no doubt that, for most members of this particular scheme, the basis of neighbourliness is a well-understood "norm of reciprocity"; being a Good Neighbour is a way of activating the norm. Many of the problems of Good Neighbour Schemes in matching help to need are at bottom a question of striking the balance of reciprocity that will make helping worthwhile.

## 2   Reaching, Yorkshire

Reaching is a mainly residential area about 2½ miles from the centre of a large northern city. In shape it is a rough triangle, bounded on two sides by major roads out of the city and on the third by open parkland. The housing stock is very mixed, although most of it was built between 1880 and 1914. Running downhill from the park are row after row of large terraced houses, succeeded nearer the city centre by much smaller terraced houses without gardens, interspersed with occasional clusters of inter-war semis. Cutting a wedge through the district is Sharp Rise, an area of broad streets and avenues of substantial, well-maintained houses with gardens and abundant trees. The social mixture parallels the housing mixture. Up to fifteen years ago, Reaching could have been described as a fairly homogeneous "respectable" working-class area surrounding a more prosperous middle-class enclave. Diversity and mobility are now the outstanding characteristics of its approximately 10,000 inhabitants. Many of the houses near the park have been divided into flats and bed-sitting rooms, occupied predominantly by students, immigrants, old people and low-income families. Further in, the houses of Sharp Rise have been largely taken over by young professional middle-class families, lecturers, social workers, actors and executives from the entertainment industries. Here the surviving working-class families, many of them elderly couples or widows, are increasingly surrounded by the removal vans, the glamorous or decrepit motor cars and the children of a very different social group. Everyone we interviewed agreed that Reaching was a very "mixed area"; one resident described it as "our Islington". It is very much the kind of area where one would expect social problems to be rampant and good neighbourliness to be conspicuous by its absence.

The Reaching Good Neighbour Scheme is a by-product of the Reaching Community Association. Both have their base firmly in the Sharp Rise area. The Community Association was formed to fight local authority plans to demolish some of the terraces and the local school; the association has enjoyed considerable success, and its general aims are to conserve the residential environment – especially that of Sharp Rise itself – and to extend the provision of such amenities as playgrounds, telephone boxes and youth clubs. The raising of community consciousness was seen as an essential step towards this goal; with that in mind, volunteers run a community shop "to help enquirers to know and claim their rights" and a community newspaper. The association's leaders see it as very much a project for *all* residents – a sentiment that gave rise to the Good Neighbour Scheme.

Peter Jarvis, a leading member of the Community Association, first suggested a Good Neighbour Scheme and later became its organiser and moving spirit. His motives were various. On the one hand, he wished to make the association more representative of the whole community, and on the other, he had a deep personal belief in the importance of neighbourliness. When his sister was a child she had one day found their next-door neighbour lying dead on his kitchen floor – a shocking experience that he cited to explain his commitment to neighbourliness. How terrible it would have been, he said, if the old man had been lying there for weeks without anyone knowing, instead of for hours; how much better if he had not had to die alone at all. Mr Jarvis grew up in a small rural community in Scotland where there were strong local, occupational and religious ties, and where good neighbours were taken for granted. His parents and their family had never left the village that was the entire world to them; but by contrast, his own generation of the family was scattered all over the world, leaving his parents alone in their old age. This situation, which he considered symptomatic of modern society as a whole, made it imperative for him to work towards creating new forms of neighbourliness. For months he and his wife had informally encouraged neighbourly helping in their immediate locality (like so many Reaching residents their local history must be measured in months rather than years). These activities eventually became too much for them to handle on their own, so Mr Jarvis suggested that they might be taken over by the Community Association. The Jarvises were by any standard active, talented people with considerable organising abilities, deeply committed to the idea of making Reaching the kind of caring community that they believed in.

Volunteers were recruited to the scheme through three different channels; they were, as a result, of three distinct types, and were used by Mr Jarvis in three distinct ways. First, there were his immediate friends and neighbours; people like himself who lived nearby and who were persuaded to become Good Neighbours because of their relationship with him and his wife. Secondly, there were those who became involved because they were members of the Community Association; most of them young middle-class people previously known to Mr Jarvis, although not in his circle of close friends. Finally, there were those recruited as the result of a questionnaire distributed to Reaching residents by the association. By these means, a total of 90 registered Good Neighbours were recruited: 12 because they were friends and neighbours of Mr Jarvis, 7 because they were members of the association, and the remainder through the questionnaire. In other words, the scheme seems to have achieved considerable success in expanding an initially localised exercise in good neighbouring into a diverse, community-wide network of Good Neighbours. That, however, is not the whole story.

The initial development of the scheme was carefully thought out. The area covered by the scheme was divided into small sections of a few streets, each with its own group of volunteers and a "supervisor" or "warden" responsible for co-ordinating their efforts and for recruiting more volunteers. Nine people said they were willing to take on this supervisory responsibility, and thus Reaching as a whole might have been covered by a localised Good Neighbour network. In practice, however, things did not work out like that. Mr Jarvis frankly admitted that, for him, one of the attractions of the scheme was the opportunity it offered for organisation and planning; he liked to keep the whole of Reaching under his eye by means of a file containing cards on all the scheme's "cases". But the decentralised arrangement meant that too little information came his way, and that problems were referred directly to the local supervisors. As a result, he as overall organiser lost touch with the community. He therefore abandoned the network system in favour of one by which he received all referrals directly and then assigned cases to volunteers. This decision did result in a scheme that was, within limits, highly successful; but those limits were set by the amount of work that the organiser could handle personally. It also meant that the vast majority of cases were referred to only one of the three types of volunteer within the scheme, those who had been the organiser's friends and neighbours to begin with; many volunteers recruited in other ways had never been used. The strong professional and organisational emphasis within this scheme is undeniably impressive. The fact that Mr Jarvis spoke of "referrals", "cases" and "supervisors", and kept an impeccably-ordered master file on almost all aspects of the scheme, placed the project firmly on the formal, bureaucratic side of social care rather than on the informal, "neighbourly" side. Yet, paradoxically, the crucial problem of the scheme was that organisationally it had not grown beyond the relationships between the organiser and his own neighbours.

Most referrals reached the organiser by telephone. The majority of them were, in fact, referrals in the strictest sense, made by the Divisional Social Services office. Although doctors, hospitals and churches had been told of the existence of the scheme, they rarely made use of it. Of 70 cases referred since September 1976, 37 had come from the Social Services, six from medical or church sources, seven seem to have been self-referrals in response to the scheme's publicity, and the remaining 22 were made by the scheme's own volunteers or by members of the Community Association. Not surprisingly, the scheme was seen as essentially a back-up service for the "welfare", both by its own members and by local Social Services staff. The Voluntary Liaison Officer who made most of the referrals did, however, ensure that the cases she referred to Mr Jarvis were, in her judgment, "within the scope" of the scheme; otherwise, she referred them directly to appropriate volunteers known to her personally and not to the scheme. This, of course, meant that the scheme came to specialise in certain types of cases – mostly those involving specific care-giving for limited periods of time. Whether the VLO was justified in thinking that this was the kind of work best suited to the members of the scheme is a moot point. She was certainly criticised on occasions by Mr Jarvis for sending him cases that were "beyond the capabilities" of his helpers. But the clearest evidence for the volunteers' preference for strictly limited commitments, and for those of "sociable" rather than "caring" nature, came from the volunteers themselves. On first making contact with the organiser, volunteers complete a questionnaire indicating the type of work they would be prepared to do. The answers speak for themselves:

| Task | In Evening | During Day |
|---|---|---|
| Offer hospitality to newcomer | 39 | 27 |
| Emergency shopping | 38 | 31 |
| Changing library books | 31 | 27 |
| Visit an elderly or sick person | 23 | 19 |
| Sit in with an invalid | 15 | 11 |
| Provide outings for handicapped | 10 | 10 |

The popularity of offering hospitality to newcomers is not surprising. Like Mr Jarvis, the active members joined the scheme as much as anything else to find friends and neighbours for themselves; the project was an exercise in "instant community" as far as they were concerned. Given their mobility and their predominantly managerial/professional occupations, it is hardly surprising that they should have used organisational methods to create the types of social relationships usually thought of as the very opposite of formal organisation. Nor, perhaps, that one of the most striking features of the scheme was its apparent under-use by the community as a whole.

When Mr Jarvis received requests for care he passed them on to his volunteers in the way he saw fit. Of this pool of 90 or more helpers, he had during a period of eighteen months called on only 42; of these, only eight had been asked to help more than once. All but two of those eight volunteers were Sharp Rise residents and all but three were part of the organiser's immediate circle of friends and neighbours. In other words, the basis of the scheme was a small active nucleus that vigorously monopolised the provision of care, rather than diffusing it through the much larger membership of the scheme. Various reasons were given for this concentration of effort. Mr Jarvis preferred to use people he knew he could rely on. Many of the cases were very urgent and he needed to be able to call on someone immediately to hand. His friends and neighbours happened to have specialist skills that made them uniquely qualified to deal with many cases that arose in this cosmopolitan area: thus, one request for help demanded an Urdu-speaking Good Neighbour, and an anthropologist friend just happened to have Urdu; another neighbour spoke fluent Spanish; yet another was once a full-time social worker and thus "knows the ropes" when obtaining support from the statutory services. Yet, behind these perfectly good reasons for the scheme's restriction of activity were signs of a more profound explanation; in an important sense, the point and value of this Good Neighbour Scheme was to develop neighbourliness among the core members, not by giving help to each other (most of them hardly needed it) but by jointly helping others. At the same time, they neither needed to – nor quite knew how to – get to know those they helped; it was not for nothing that they thought of them as "cases".

The under-use of the scheme had three aspects. Few of the people referred to the Good Neighbours developed any real relationship with the volunteers. Most of the volunteers had either never been asked to do anything by the organiser or felt that they had been asked to do too little. And the scheme had no contact with – and its existence was probably unknown to – the majority of the population in the area that it claimed to serve. Thus, of all the cases referred to the scheme, only 11 had come to be classified by the organiser as "long-term"; that is to say, in only 11 instances had the initial visit grown into a sustained caring relationship, into "neighbourliness". It was noticeable, too, that none of the volunteers who had become involved in these long-term relationships were members of the scheme's "core group", but belonged to the majority that had come into the scheme in response to the questionnaire – people who do not live in Sharp Rise and for whom Mr Jarvis was little more than "a voice on the telephone". Few of the long-term cases had been identified as such when they first came to Mr Jarvis' attention; they began as limited requests for help and became something more thereafter, as a result of the accident of being passed to one of the "questionnaire" volunteers. These volunteers had apparently *chosen* to transform their cases into relationships. By contrast, almost all the calls for help initially judged by Mr Jarvis to imply long-term support had been regretfully rejected by him as being unsuitable for his volunteers.

The same imbalance emerged even more strikingly when we interviewed the volunteers themselves. With hardly an exception, they complained that the scheme did not give them enough to do: "I haven't been asked often enough"; "I joined the scheme thinking it would be a way of getting to know people – you know, we're all newcomers here – but so far I've only been given this one old lady to visit". Most of the volunteers are indeed new-comers to Reaching, having lived there for less than five years. Most of them are under 35, and were quite explicit about their own need for neighbours: "As I understand it, the idea is to help people to get to know each other, to break down barriers; it's badly needed in an area like this, people move around so much and the natural networks get broken down"; "In a mixed area like this there's not that much contact, it's a way for people to meet and help each other"; "It puts people in touch; everyone has needs; the scheme tries to make it a two-way thing – you help with the shopping, they help with the baby-sitting": "I thought it would be a marvellous way of making friends locally". For some, the scheme had indeed worked that way although the friends they have made have been other volunteers or members of the scheme rather than clients – few of them had made more than one brief visit or performed more than one particular service for the scheme's clients. These were the volunteers already caught up in the organiser's personal social network or in other projects of the Community Association. For them, the scheme had succeeded in consolidating a network of friends and neighbours, even though it was one in which the "cases" to whom they gave short-term care had no real part: "It's like having a family; the natural structures of the family have broken down but that doesn't mean to say they can't be re-structured; with the scheme you know there's a lot of very supportive people around; we are not local people, only one of our friends is, so we depend on each other in the same way that people who have family nearby do"; "We really have made friends, you know, it's a funny thing, this area, my husband's a bus driver, next door there's a probation officer, then a lecturer; on the other side there's a retired housekeeper; there's not many who were born and bred here, but we've all become very friendly; if I wanted to talk to someone there's at least twelve doors I could knock on for a cup of coffee; yes, I think the scheme's done a lot".

At the other extreme, however, were the majority of volunteers for whom the scheme had conspicuously failed to overcome isolation, either by giving them the opportunity to develop caring relationships with their neighbours, or by drawing them into the busy, friendly world revolving around Mr Jarvis. These are the people who joined in response to the questionnaire; for them, remoteness has not been alleviated by their membership: "I don't think I know anyone else in the scheme; I take this old lady who's blind out

71

shopping once a week and that's it; Mr Jarvis is just a name to me"; "Well, I can't tell you what the scheme is doing really; I visit an old man down the road and do odd jobs for him, but I've no idea about the others; Mr Jarvis' name is always in the papers but personally I wouldn't know him if I saw him"; "I'm sorry, I don't know anyone else who's in the scheme". It is these Good Neighbours, isolated from the core group, who not only emphasise the importance of localised networks of neighbourliness but have also turned their own work for the scheme into long-term relationships with their "cases": "The scheme would be more successful if it were more to do with the neighbours who are just around you and not streets away . . . this is a long street and I only know five people; the rest is let off in flats so you never know who is who"; "I think if it were run more locally that would help"; "Well, I was sent to see this old couple and I go three or four times a week now, shopping, painting, listening to their troubles, he's very bad with arthritis and I think she's on the verge of a nervous breakdown, she has hallucinations. I'm sure something ought to be done for them, but I don't know who to go to. I phoned Mr Jarvis twice about them but he never phoned back". Perhaps the commonest problem among this group of volunteers is a sense of isolation. Members of the scheme had, for example, never been given an opportunity to meet as a group to discuss their work: "I think there should be meetings for the volunteers"; "If only we could all get together and meet Mr Jarvis"; "If we could share some of these problems — perhaps one of the other volunteers could advise me on what my old lady's entitled to"; "There ought to be meetings". Thus, a neighbourly scheme has developed within the larger scheme: in the process, a widespread neighbourliness has been sacrificed to the efficient delivery of specific services.

## 3 Task Force, Greenwich

Task Force is an organisation principally concerned with supporting pensioners. On several occasions, however, it has been drawn into a more general encouragement of local neighbourliness, finding that to be *the best way in practice of securing the narrower objective*. Stephen Faulkner has described one such instance in Greenwich. In September 1976 the Greenwich Task Force Centre appointed a Neighbourhood Worker and gave him an open brief: "Basically, the idea was to be a mixture of traditional work methods (especially the matching of individual volunteers to pensioners) and the general aims of Community Development (the encouragement of a more caring neighbourhood)." Faced on the one hand with a steep increase in social work referrals in certain localities, and on the other with problems of recruiting enough volunteers in those areas, the Neighbourhood Worker was simply given the task of "getting inside" these difficult neighbourhoods to discover what opportunities there were to "help in tackling some of the problems which pensioners faced". After three months of quiet exploration, one of these neighbourhoods, Barnfield Gardens, was chosen for concentrated attention. Like the other areas, it had a high incidence of social work referrals, a dearth of resident volunteers and a bad reputation for neighbourliness. In addition, it had a high proportion of pensioners among its residents. The area itself, a large council estate surrounded by private housing, was geographically well-defined, and it had a "point of entry" for the Task Force Worker in the shape of an established Tenants' Association. This last factor, the existence of an active community organisation, seems to have been the key to what eventually happened.

The Neighbourhood Worker started out with a difficult dilemma. On the one hand, the day-to-day needs of the Barnfield pensioners had to be met, and on the other, arrangements had to be worked out to enable residents to provide that care for themselves. They also had to be worked out quickly and with limited resources: although Task Force saw neighbourhood work as "about developing the community itself, both to identify its problems and to take steps towards solving them", it simply did not have the means to do this from scratch in an area such as Barnfield. The Task Force Worker had to choose between trying to develop a Neighbourhood Care Scheme of the kind he thought appropriate, and making what use he could of existing local organisations, "however inappropriate they may have seemed at the time", in order to solve at least some of the immediate problems of the elderly. Eventually, the decision was made on a pragmatic basis. The Tenants' Association already existed, and was well-placed to deal with some of the most pressing of the pensioners' problems, such as the repair of flats. From the Worker's point of view, it was necessary to solve such problems as best he could rather than take the time to develop entirely new organisations. Hence, the decision to turn to the Association seemed inevitable.

To begin with, however, the Association was not particularly keen to be drawn into neighbourhood care. Despite its activities and its useful outside contacts, it had "like many of the Tenants' Associations which came into prominence in the fight against the Housing Finance Act . . . become very inward-looking and had concentrated its resources on more social activities". Stephen Faulkner describes its response:

An initial approach to the Association was met with very mixed feelings. Some members shared the view that the Association should be responding to the needs of their elderly members and encouraging them to play a more active part in the activities of the Association. However, the dominant view was "ageist" in the extreme. "Pensioners have too much done for them as it is"; "Nearly all their pensions go on bingo. I know, I've seen them", were just two of the many comments made.

73

It was all very well for the Neighbourhood Worker to decide that neighbourhood schemes should be based on local community organisations because of their contacts, networks and credibility. But what if the local community organisation wasn't interested – or if members with "ageist" attitudes were actively opposed? While seeking a solution to this problem, the Task Force Worker found that he was frequently asked to describe exactly what he was doing on the estate. Not wanting to fall back into the position of being simply the local Task Force officer, but without any firm plans for a neighbourhood care scheme, he settled for the rather vague but forward-looking formula: "We are trying to get pensioners and others together on the estate to see if they are having common problems, and then see if there is anything that we can do together about it". On that basis, and backed by the support of a growing number of individual residents whose "referrals" he had taken up, as well as that of some local councillors, the Worker gradually wore down the distrust of certain members of the Tenants' Association. He felt eventually that he had gathered enough support to risk a second formal approach to the Association. He did not propose any specific caring activity, but merely "a very simple survey of the estate", to be carried out by himself, members of the Association's committee and some of the more active pensioners. He emphasised that the survey would not only gather information about pensioners' problems but might also encourage new residents to join the Association.

The survey was indeed "very simple". It consisted of four questions: "Name and Address? Are you a member of the Tenants' Association? If not, why not? Have you any major problems?" Even though it was never in fact completed, this survey had an electrifying effect on the Association's committee. While carrying out the survey, members of the committee encountered at first-hand the problems of their elderly neighbours. And usually, having reached that point, "they would take it upon themselves to try and sort the problems out". This was where the established networks and contacts of the Association were so valuable: they not only knew how to get problems solved, but also, when faced with official delays and evasions, how to find alternative resources. "Because of their contacts (family, work and friends) or physical fitness, they were able to chase up alternatives. They would get someone in to repair a fault rather than wait around for the Council. Pensioners by and large did not have these options". As a result of the survey, then, things began to happen – and it was the leading members of the Tenants' Association who were making them happen:

At the next meeting of the Tenants' Association Committee a full report-back was made. For the first time new members of the Association attended the meeting and contributed, and an overall picture began to emerge of poor information, unsympathetic responses from statutory agencies, head-banging and frustration.

74

Some people present said that they had been appalled to realise exactly what it was like to have to live on a pension. The meeting lasted four hours!

By this time the Association was ready to commit itself wholeheartedly to neighbourhood care. The next problem (experienced in different ways by an enormous number of schemes) was to sustain and build on that momentum. Real "possibilities for the beginnings of an estate-wide Neighbourhood Care Scheme" had begun to emerge. Some of the pensioners were now members of the Association, and the Association itself was increasing its activity on behalf of the elderly.

In Stephen Faulkner's view, what kept the project moving at this stage was the possibility of absorbing the new caring activities into the well-established formal and informal "networks" developed by the Association. Even in its relatively moribund state, the Association had maintained regular contact with residents in three ways: some members collected subscriptions, others delivered the Association newsletter, and yet others ran various social activities. Getting this core of regular helpers to work with pensioners was the next essential step. Bridges had to be built: a pensioners' representative was elected to the committee; a pensioners' club was started; material about welfare rights and other questions of direct concern to the elderly was included in the newsletter; those who ran the nursery on the estate were persuaded to let grandparents visit at any time; and many other small initiatives were taken. Eventually, the point was reached when it seemed only natural for the networks of the Association to look after the needs of the elderly throughout the estate. By that time, more formal arrangements could be made: a "skills list" was compiled of residents willing to give help (although, as have many other schemes, the Barnfield project here encountered the problem of being unable to use the skills of many volunteers quickly enough to give them a genuine sense of being needed); a meeting was called (in the local pub), at which the pensioners' representative described to all the Association's helpers what they might be able to do for pensioners on the estate.

The pensioners' representative and the Task Force Worker gradually emerged as the *de facto* organisers of a Barnfield Neighbourhood Care Scheme, even though the scheme itself was largely contained within the networks of the Tenants' Association. By this time, therefore, "people with either referrals or problems of their own would come to the organisers in the initial stages, especially if specialist information was needed"; but the system was also working well in its own right as an encouragement to neighbourliness: "it was not uncommon for a newsletter deliverer to meet a pensioner, inform him or her of the next coffee evening, call round for them, introduce them to others, recruit them to the Tenants' Association, perhaps untangle a welfare rights problem and so on". The scheme still had far to go

75

before it could cover the whole estate, either in terms of information or care. Accidents, illnesses – even deaths – were a constant reminder of the gaps still to be filled. And, as the scheme became more comprehensive and reached an ever larger proportion of residents, the inevitable difficulties of personal relationships between neighbours began to crop up. Although a great deal of goodwill, skill and readiness to help was manifested, it also became clear that years of neighbouring had led to considerable ill-will, gossip and outright enmity that severely limited the potential efficacy of any informal caring scheme. Stephen Faulkner was unusually frank about this: "Good neighbourliness as idealised by the DHSS often fails to take account of such considerations. Often people just do not like one another; why should they pretend otherwise? This created enormous tensions". Thus, although the official attitudes of the Tenants' Association had changed, and although many residents had been mobilised to help one another, these very changes had revealed not only the potential but also the limitations of Good Neighbouring. Although relationships between contacts and helpers on the one hand and clients and pensioners on the other were generally stable and mutually rewarding, "personality clashes were frequent and often were of such a magnitude that some volunteers found it impossible to carry on".

After 18 months, however, there were still ample grounds for judging the project successful. On the basis of the Tenants' Association a network of caring activity had been built up that now involved the newsletter deliverers, the subscription collectors, the pensioners' club, arts and crafts classes, a large team of skilled and unskilled volunteers, block contacts throughout the estate, home helps, social workers and the Task Force Neighbourhood Worker – the latter playing a progressively less directive role. But over and above all this, "the great thing", as Stephen Faulkner wrote, "was that people *did* become more sympathetic to the needs of their friends and neighbours and their fellow helpers". It became more and more possible for him to feel that, because the Tenants' Association, as a collective interest of the residents, was at the centre of the scheme, not only were "the caring networks a secure feature of the estate", but also that the Task Force Worker might soon be withdrawn.

Eventual withdrawal is an important aspect of neighbourhood action as practised by Task Force. Their usual strategy is to go into a locality, do whatever is necessary to generate self-sustaining self-help activity and organisation among the residents, and then move on. Ideally – and the strategy is admittedly idealistic – this kind of development results in a community that is able to fight its own battles and within which Neighbourhood Care Schemes, once appropriate networks have been activated, can run themselves. At this point in the process, however, the previously remarkable success story of Barnfield began to go wrong. Task Force decided to withdraw its Neighbourhood Worker, even though it was not altogether happy about leaving things entirely to the Tenants' Association. An independent Pensioners' Action Association was set up to fill the gap, but it failed to secure the necessary support; by contrast with the discreet reinforcement of an existing community organisation that had characterised the previous two years, the attempt to introduce a brand-new body oriented towards a specific form of local social care collapsed in the face of personal and political squabbles. To Stephen Faulkner, at least, the lesson was clear. By extending the well-established contacts of a genuinely local agency, much had been done to mobilise neighbourly action – but such mobilisation needed the *continuing* support, however discreet, of a committed individual who could in effect assume a professional responsibility for the survival of the scheme. Moreover, events in Barnfield had shown that, in order to mobilise residents and hold the scheme together, as well as to maximise its ability to function as an independent local exercise in neighbourhood care, it was necessary to move away from a concern with specific client groups (in this case pensioners) and specific problems (in this case welfare rights) towards a much more comprehensive position – in effect, a readiness to take up any genuine problem or need of any resident. A team of workers with ample time and resources could perhaps have achieved more, but in practical terms the lesson of Barnfield seems to be that, for the purposes of encouraging a neighbourhood to provide its own neighbourhood care – and to do so on the basis of limited resources and a limited number of people able to offer full-time involvement (which is very much the situation of most Good Neighbour Schemes) – the combination of an existing neighbourhood organisation and a determined semi-professional who knows his way around welfare is not a bad formula. A crucial problem is to relate local concern and care to the outer world of resources, powers and services. In Barnfield, the Tenants' Association and the Task Force Worker between them were able to do this most effectively, thus overcoming one of the most frequent and disabling difficulties of less fortunate projects.

Stephen Faulkner concludes his own report on the Barnfield venture with a "balance sheet" of achievements and problems as he saw them after two years' work – that is, after not only the successful expansion of the Tenants' Association into neighbourhood care, but also the difficulties attendant on the attempt to withdraw the Neighbourhood Worker and substitute a Pensioners' Action Association. Our own experience of Barnfield suggests that his summing-up is both perceptive and, although overtly aimed towards the special concerns of Task Force, of real value for Good Neighbouring generally. So we end this case study by repeating his main conclusions.

"Over the last couple of months", he writes, "the Worker on Barnfield has played a much smaller part in the life of the estate. The ability of people working within the networks developed by the Tenants' Association to respond to problems has been fully tested. In the main local people do now respond in a much more effective and sympathetic way to the needs of the local elderly". At the same time, the Tenants' Association itself is much more directly influenced by the elderly residents of the estate, although "younger people, too, have begun to be involved in the Association, often having been recruited by pensioners who have helped sort out some small problem or other". Similarly, "local councillors and the Social Services Department respond more quickly when approached" and "the councillors have opened a weekly surgery on the estate". The Task Force Worker himself still has a crucial role, but it is very much in the background. "Of course when new problems occur the Worker is called upon, but in the main people on the estate either consult one another or get on the phone to someone who will have the information (something not many people had the confidence to do in the past)." A striking feature of the scheme, which results directly from its origins within the Tenants' Association, is its achievement of a high degree of invisibility. "Having been systematically based on the existing networks on the estate, the work on Barnfield is *extremely informal*". Thus, "if you were to ask even those centrally involved in the work (say, the pensioners' representative) she would not dream of saying that she had helped in the establishment of a Neighbourhood Care Scheme! She would be much more likely to say that she had helped beef up the Tenants' Association and helped people get to know one another and help other people. This is real strength. Because it is so informal, and people do not have little flags on their heads saying 'Block Contact', 'member of Skills List' or just 'Interested Helper,' they are much more able to help out 'naturally'. Of late some people have even asked why the Worker is on the estate". In sum, the elderly are more involved in the life of the estate, younger people are more aware of the needs of the elderly, there is closer co-operation between residents and the statutory services, especially the Home Help service, and there has been a steady spill-over of the work into more diverse kinds of involvement and caring activity. The Task Force Worker is still considered as indispensable, but his role is increasingly that of an informed outside ally who keeps in touch with the estate by visiting the pensioners' club once a fortnight and maintaining contact with one or two central figures among the residents; he is no longer the omnipresent promoter, co-ordinator, organiser and problem-solver of earlier days. The overall success of the scheme is seen to stem from both its use of existing local networks and its readiness to progress from a single purpose (help for pensioners) towards a much wider range of concerns as needs were discovered. But of course, despite all this optimism, the Barnfield project is still, as Stephen Faulkner and the Task Force Centre were all too aware, vulnerable to new problems, as any attempt to generate neighbourliness always is. The partial and phased withdrawal of the Worker had been reasonably successful, but new personality clashes could always occur;

what would happen, for example, to the scheme if the pensioners' representative moved away from the estate? If the optimistic view of the project is justified, the networks of care on the estate will prove strong enough to survive the comings and goings of individuals. This would really be success.

## 4 Sheffield

In most English cities and counties the local authorities, together with the major voluntary organisations such as Age Concern, the WRVS and the churches, have developed reasonably comprehensive and effective systems of neighbourhood care, providing all kinds of emergency and visiting arrangements, clubs and domiciliary services. Over the years, a complex web of care has been built up. In such a setting, there can often seem to be little or no need for new initiatives to encourage neighbourly relationships as well as caring services. Many authorities and organisations appear to have taken the view that neighbourhood care – in the sense of delivering appropriate help and support to people in their own homes and localities and, when necessary, transporting those people from their homes and localities to wherever expert services are available – can be achieved quite satisfactorily by existing statutory and voluntary methods, without the added complication of grass-roots projects that are also interested in making neighbourhoods more "neighbourly". Patch social work and various forms of community work are obvious examples of ways in which neighbourhood care can be strengthened without necessarily becoming involved in strengthening neighbourliness as well. The authorities that have decided that existing services can cope adequately with the additional need to provide neighbourhood care may well be right. Yet, in some cities and counties a rather more positive effort to combine neighbourhood care with neighbourliness seems to have been made; the need for neighbourhood care has, in such cases, been more or less deliberately linked to the call for social policy to make room for neighbourliness. The results of our survey suggest that Sheffield is a good example of such a response.

We were initially rather depressed by Sheffield. For a city of its size it seemed to have remarkably few Good Neighbour Schemes; in fact, we were unable to discover a single scheme independent of the old-established voluntary organisations or of the statutory services. But, on closer examination, we realised that this apparent dearth of independent schemes did not reflect either an indifference to Good Neighbouring among the city's voluntary and statutory bodies or a "saturation" of the community by efficient professional caring services, but rather a situation in which the promotion of neighbourliness had indeed been seriously taken up, but *inside* the framework of the existing statutory and voluntary system. To simplify matters a good deal, what has happened in Sheffield is that the local authority and the local churches have between them made a substantial effort to make room for Good Neighbouring within their own structures and services. The effect – about which very different political judgements could be made – has been that, on the one hand, there is little evidence of an independent Good Neighbour movement in Sheffield, but on the other hand the cultivation of neighbourliness and support for neighbourly helping has become an important activity for a wide range of official and voluntary social services. For better or worse, Good Neighbouring has been incorporated into the system of voluntary and statutory social care. We shall here discuss just two aspects of this situation: the community care programme of the churches, and the home warden service of the local authority. Taken together, they seem to us to make a substantial contribution towards solving the problem of combining support for neighbourliness with reliable, comprehensive and localised caring services. Whether it is a solution everyone will accept is another matter. Nor do we claim that Sheffield is unique, or that its response to the problem is the only feasible one; we merely suggest that it is one of the few places where a possible solution has been thoroughly tested in practice. We do not even suggest that the Sheffield solution was achieved in any very conscious or deliberate way. But, earlier in this report, we have argued that, however paradoxical it may seem, positive support from existing statutory and voluntary agencies appears to be a vital condition for the successful encouragement of neighbourliness through Good Neighbouring – and the pattern of social care in Sheffield is simply one instance of how such encouragement might be given. In that sense, places like Sheffield differ dramatically from other cities and counties – such as Birmingham or West Sussex – where an equal effort has been made to promote neighbourhood care, but where neighbourliness has simply not been put on the agenda of neighbourhood care to the same extent.

Our first approach in Sheffield, as in all other areas, was to the local Social Services Department. Rather than describing its own official activities, the Department drew our attention to the partnership between its Family and Community Services Division and the voluntary and informal provision of care in the city. Specifically:

"The main schemes are those organised by the Churches' Council for Community Care. The CCCC has two forms of Good Neighbour Scheme. The Good Neighbour 'Liaison' Scheme was started fourteen years ago by local churches in conjunction with social work staff. The Good Neighbour 'Contact' Scheme was started more recently, in response to overtures from this Department. In addition to these schemes, neighbourly help is provided on a more local and less formal basis by churches, tenants' and community associations and voluntary organisations such as the League of the Good Samaritan. Unfortunately, it is not practical to collate all this information, but our divisional teams endeavour to keep in touch with the appropriate bodies in their respective localities".

On the strength of this, we next contacted the Churches' Council for Community Care. The Council, set up in 1966, is a complex alliance between religious welfare agencies and the statutory authorities for the purpose of co-ordinating and supporting neighbourhood care and Good Neighbouring. All the main Christian denominations are involved (but no non-Christian ones) together with the local Social Services Department, the Probation Service, the Area Health Authority and the principal Christian voluntary organisations such as the Society of St Vincent de Paul, the Mothers' Union, the Salvation Army and the Methodist Fellowship.

At the time of our survey, the Council received a local authority grant of £4,600 and a further £1,100 of small grants from other sources. Most of this income was used to staff, equip and run a small headquarters office, from which three paid workers co-ordinated a large and complicated network of projects throughout the Sheffield Metropolitan District. The object of the Council, as described by its Chairman, is to "inspire every neighbourhood in our city to be a 'good neighbourhood', a place where people naturally care and take thought for one another".

The Council sponsors and organises three main types of neighbourhood care. In addition to the "Liaison" and "Contact" schemes already mentioned, there is a group of "Community Care Volunteers" responsible for meeting certain kinds of need that the Good Neighbour Schemes could not handle on their own. The three ventures must be viewed as a single programme – and as a programme that is closely bound up with official services – if the work of the explicitly "Good Neighbour" projects is to be fully appreciated. In Sheffield, it is well understood that no one type of person, project or organisation can hope to deal with the whole range of needs for neighbourly help that arise in a neighbourhood and that, accordingly, an alliance of many diverse and complementary schemes is needed to achieve adequate care and heightened neighbourliness.

The Good Neighbour Liaison Scheme that operates throughout the city is, in fact, a network of localised and, in many respects, largely autonomous schemes, which nevertheless each follow "the same recognised basic pattern" of activity and organisation. Each local scheme has an unpaid Liaison Officer appointed by the Churches Council with responsibility for a specified area, within which he or she is "prepared to receive calls for help from statutory workers, hospitals, doctors, clergy, domiciliary services and other organisations" and then to find suitable local helpers to take on the necessary work. The Liaison Officers are obviously the key people in the schemes, since it is they who link together those who need help or care, those who are willing and able to give it, and the various social service and medical agencies to which the need for help is initially made known or to

81

which needs for specialised professional services will eventually be referred. The original aim of the scheme was to offer all the kinds of help "which any friend or neighbour can provide". Although volunteers were not to be asked "to undertake any job for which they did not feel competent", the range of work envisaged was nevertheless very wide, including: "friendly visiting of old people or invalids living alone; occasional practical help for elderly or infirm people, such as shopping, warming-up light meals at times when the home help service or Meals on Wheels are not available, or bridging the gap when someone is discharged from hospital; help to mothers, such as visiting a sick child in hospital or looking after children while the mother visits a child in hospital; visiting hospital patients whose friends or relations live too far away to come and see them; providing transport to Day Centres, acting as escort for out-patients attending hospitals [and generally meeting the] increasing need for day-time transport".

In practice, the scheme's activities have been more limited. At the time of our survey, there were 48 Liaison Officers in post throughout seven "divisions" of the city, and the returns made by 42 of them showed that, during the six months up to June 1976, 452 helpers had been available to the local schemes and that 313 new requests for help had been dealt with. The returns also showed that the schemes were considerably more numerous, better supported and more active in some divisions of the city than in others (for example, 14 Liaison Officers, 231 helpers and 158 new requests for help in Division 3, compared with 2 Liaison Officers, 8 helpers and 5 new calls for help in Division 6). The evidence suggested that the areas where schemes were weakest were, in fact, those where the need for help might be greatest – the fact that the number of calls for help appears to increase with the number of volunteers available means that one cannot assume an absence of need in areas where the schemes are weak. No less worrying is the difficulty reported to us by several Liaison Officers in recruiting or retaining helpers for some of the tasks that the schemes expected to take on – in particular, day-time transport and long-term visiting. In some areas of the city, we were flatly told that "long-term visiting is impossible". The scarcity of volunteers, especially those able to offer day-time transport, was generally attributed to the fact that so many women worked – particularly in areas where need was presumed to be the greatest. Thus, although the Liaison Scheme was thought to be "working satisfactorily", there was a clear recognition that, for practical purposes, the kinds of help that "*any* friend or neighbour can provide" are restricted – largely by the demands of everyday life on the time of most friends and neighbours, but perhaps also because, "as we say in Yorkshire, nobody will do owt for nowt".

The feeling seems to have been that, although the rewards need not necessarily be financial, there should at least be *some* rewards. As one Liaison Officer put it: "I think if more people would spare a few hours each week to help someone in need, the community would be better all round; but it's a lifelong job. Because it's no good doing something for a couple of weeks then tiring of it; the person who is being helped will begin the week looking forward to someone's company. I visit a depressed lady, not a pensioner, who needs someone to talk to for a couple of hours each week. She is housebound, but I have to be back home to see to my children at dinner time. I go on the bus and come back by bus, but in going to see her I've made a new friend with whom I have a laugh and a chat. I wouldn't want to stop going now". Perhaps breaking the "nobody will do owt for nowt" pattern in that way should be numbered among the crucial administrative problems for schemes of this type. Once again, it is a question of matching need and care, of understanding the ways in which helpers can assist each other.

The Community Care Volunteers project was launched at least partly to meet the need for long-term visiting and specialised help that was proving beyond the capacity of the Liaison Scheme; specifically, it was to recruit people "who could give long-term help to people known to be facing difficult personal and material problems". By 1977, a team of 92 volunteers had been built up throughout the city. The volunteers are given a short course of training and then work in close collaboration with professional social workers, probation officers or other statutory staff. Once again, the concept of the local resident as a responsible but informal link between those in need of help and the official agencies is stressed; "the idea is for volunteers to keep their spontaneity, which will enable them to relate more to the clients and not to turn them into mini-probation officers". Nevertheless, for quite a number of volunteers one attraction of the scheme seems to have been the fact that it could provide a means of entry into full-time social work. The central problem here – apart from simply recruiting enough volunteers – is to preserve the balance between the volunteers' leanings towards professional social work and their value as agents of more "neighbourly" social care. This problem has perhaps been particularly acute in Sheffield because of the extent to which the Community Care Volunteers have been used at the fringes of professional social work to provide neighbourly support for offenders, illiterates and people involved in matrimonial cases, as well as for a wide range of less formal helping.

Contrasting with and complementing the Council's first two schemes is the most recent, the Good Neighbour "Contact" Scheme. This is emphatically directed towards the ordinary residents of Sheffield rather than the array of service-providing agencies. Once again, there is a strong emphasis on neighbourliness, but whereas the Liaison Scheme is designed to help clients "found" by the social and medical services, the Contact Scheme depends on the direct monitoring of need among neighbours; the project's slogan is "Will You Keep Your Eyes Open?" The main role of the "Contacts", of whom at the time of our survey there were 390 covering 235 streets and 7 blocks of flats, is preventative, a matter of having "in every road, street or block of flats in the city . . . someone willing to keep their eyes open on a few houses in their neighbourhood for any signs of emergency . . . so that anyone in difficulty has someone near at hand who is in touch with the people who can help." Often, of course, the Contacts themselves give help, but their basic responsibility is to know their neighbours sufficiently well to detect possible needs and to ensure that appropriate caring services are informed in good time. To facilitate this, almost all the Contacts are grouped into 20 "schemes", each with a co-ordinating secretary; central co-ordination is carried out by the SCCCC office, thus ensuring a comprehensive flow of information. When we made our enquiries, 365 of the Contacts were thus incorporated into local schemes, and a further 25 (responsible for 25 streets) were unattached. The presence of these unattached Good Neighbours is one sign of the possible limits to the kind of highly-structured caring system that the SCCCC would like to achieve. It had become clear that the variable success of the Council's projects in different parts of the city was partly the result not of an absence of neighbourliness but of a reluctance on the part of local residents to 'link up' with larger, semi-official organisations. All the Council's ventures are, after all, quite closely controlled; in the Contact Scheme, one obvious manifestation of this is the requirement "we feel it necessary to make so as to safeguard the scheme from abuse . . . that every volunteer should be able to supply a reference, the name of one person already involved in community care work, or some well established member of the community". Such perfectly sensible safeguards cannot, unfortunately, help but give the scheme a colouring of somewhat "un-neighbourly" control.

On the whole, the Churches Council has been sensitive to such difficulties. It has demonstrated an increasing flexibility by attempting to live with these problems while at the same time expanding the coverage of its schemes: "After all, our job is not to impose our solutions and ideas . . . if the ones we would normally recommend appear inappropriate to those on the spot". An enquiry carried out by the Council in 1977 went even further in stressing the need for flexibility: "Previously", as the Chairman put it, "We have tried to build up basic general patterns, acceptable in many neighbourhoods. Where these patterns have met a negative response, it is often because people believe that they already have in existence alternative methods of working which are at least as effective and are more natural to the people concerned". At this kind of frontier, perhaps, the type of city-wide co-ordination envisaged by the Council could go no further than a discreet attempt to "know what is going on". Similarly, it was found that in many areas the boundaries between the Liaison and Contact Schemes were hard to preserve; members of the Liaison Scheme were drifting into doing the work assigned for Contacts and, conversely, Contacts were going beyond monitoring into practical caring activities; there was a general "move towards overlapping ground". Here, the response has been to continue formal sponsorship of both types of scheme as separate ventures, but to allow in practice distinctions to be blurred in certain areas. Now that some sort of presence has been achieved throughout the city, the tendency is to allow the formal structures of Good Neighbouring to adapt to the informal conventions of neighbourliness.

Meanwhile, in the more formal regions of social care, the city's Good Neighbour Schemes receive vital support from several statutory services that have themselves moved towards "neighbourly" action. The example we have chosen is that of the Home Warden Service; although we must again stress that, in discussing the SCCCC projects and the Home Warden Service, we are only exemplifying what *might* be done by statutory and voluntary agencies to create a favourable environment for neighbourhood care – it is in no sense a detailed prescription for what would need to be done elsewhere.

The Sheffield Home Warden Service began in 1963 with 20 full-time wardens, and has steadily expanded to reach its present establishment of 187. The concept of a warden service was introduced when it became clear that the Home Help Service did not provide adequate cover for clients and that informal care alone could not sufficiently supplement its work. It was felt that some elderly people needed less extensive help more frequently, in the evenings and at weekends as well as during the day. The warden service was intended to operate at all hours and to complement the Home Help Service in providing a complete domiciliary caring service; the wardens would undertake the more personal duties, whilst the Home Helps tackled the more concentrated, time-consuming tasks. Many wardens said that their motives to taking the job included a desire to do more for their clients than simply clean for them.

The duties of the wardens are described in a Departmental leaflet:

"The wardens work a 40 hour week, mainly in the mornings and evenings and over the weekend on a rota system. As far as possible they work in pairs or sometimes in a group of three to provide relief for each other in times of sickness and during holiday periods. Twelve part-time wardens have been appointed to assist certain groups where there are particular difficulties. All wardens live within the area in which they work and most clients live within five to ten minutes of their home. Each warden assists approximately 25 people, some of whom require calls three times per day, once a day, twice weekly, and some are only visited once per week. Frequency of visiting and duties are discussed by the warden and home help organiser weekly. *A general interpretation of their duties is that they will carry out the more personal services such as would be given by an only daughter,* for example helping people to get up and dress, lighting fires, giving

85

meals, writing letters, helping to wash them or being on hand when the bath is taken. They do collect pensions and small amounts of shopping. In some cases where the client is confused, the home warden will be responsible for managing her income, keeping strict accounts for checking with the Organiser weekly. In some measure it is hoped that the wardens foster a community spirit and self help amongst the people themselves.

Wardens receive special training, particularly in simple first aid, lifting of bedfast clients, physical and mental health of the elderly, practical health care, nutrition and budgeting, and home safety. Wardens are also encouraged to look out for anyone who may be in need within their area and to give the necessary attention required in an emergency. It is necessary to keep a balance between the various types of clients so the demand on the warden does not become unreasonable. The weekly rate of pay is £62.43 plus 60p allowance for incidental expenses. All wardens are on the telephone. Wardens are issued with overalls, mac, shopping basket, *protection buzzer*. Sheets, flasks and hot water bottles are available at the Divisional Office in case of need."

Almost all the wardens (175 out of 187) were recruited from the Home Help Service, thus ensuring that their backgrounds and abilities were known to their employers. The Divisional Home Help Organiser mentioned three qualities that she looked for when selecting wardens: good health, literacy and a "gleam of caring qualities". She said that this latter quality could be recognised intuitively at the interview, and that it was most likely to be found among those who had had some of "life's experiences" – by which she meant marriage and the raising of a family. She preferred to employ wardens who do not simply perform their duties, but also care emotionally for their clients.

All the wardens meet fortnightly at the office to discuss problems with the organisers and with the other wardens. This meeting provides positive group reinforcement for wardens, particularly those newly-appointed ones who might be unsure of their role, or who are feeling the adverse effects of neighbourhood gossip. The Organiser said that the wardens were by no means always seen as "saints" in the neighbourhoods where they worked; dislike of the clients, or jealousy of the services offered to them, could result, in some sections of the community, in considerable criticism of the wardens. This was particularly likely in the more deprived areas, where most of the clients were people at risk who probably did not have familial or neigh-bourly help, but where there were also people in similar circumstances who, although they did benefit from informal care, were indignant that they were not receiving the same state benefits as the clients. This attitude could be disseminated through the neighbourhood networks of which the instigator of the complaints was a part. Hence, the visit of a warden could *increase* a client's isolation from the rest of the community, understandably leading the warden to question her role as a "carer for the lonely and needy". But the Organiser stressed that these were only isolated instances. Generally speaking, there was considerable goodwill in the community towards the warden scheme – a verdict supported by our own observations in the field.

It was these direct observations that enabled us, more than anything else, to observe how a statutory service run by people for whom efficiency, accountability and, in the Organiser's words, a "super-oiled office machinery with everything at hand" are the keys to success, could nevertheless provide an effective environment for authentic neighbourly care.

The daily routine of the wardens – the fact that they work within a few minutes' walk of their own homes and are thus genuine neighbours, sharing the same local world as their clients – seemed to us in case after case to provide a firm basis for the growth of personal and sincere caring relationships. Having interviewed many of the wardens and accompanied some of them on their rounds, we concluded that the "gleam of caring qualities" had often transformed their work into a form of neighbourly care based on local knowledge and a genuine attachment to the hundreds of isolated people in Sheffield whose needs for long-term and semi-skilled care had put them beyond the capacities of the less formal Good Neighbour Schemes but who were both able and anxious to stay at home rather than enter an institution. Again and again, we found that the wardens' regular visits, and the simple tasks they carried out, had led to solid friendships and involvements (even though the wardens sometimes told us "you can't afford to become involved"). The wardens' local knowledge has led to their involvement in caring activities over and above those officially assigned to them, and many of them had become known, liked and trusted throughout their neighbourhoods. We were not surprised, therefore, when clients spoke of their wardens as friends, neighbours or even more: "I don't call her 'Home Warden' or 'Mrs', I call her Alice and she's my angel".

In sum, if Sheffield can be regarded as having solved, at least in principle, the problem of combining neighbourhood care with the encouragement of neighbourliness, it is because of the battery of complementary schemes and arrangements that the voluntary and statutory bodies have combined to foster. An overall framework of support has been constructed, within which local initiatives can be taken, but which ensures reliability and accountability of service.

## 5   Hope Green Good Neighbours, Camden

The Hope Green Good Neighbours Scheme is one of a number of voluntary schemes that operate in Camden under the "umbrella" of the Borough's own Neighbourhood Care Service. Its peculiar problems and its modest success can both be seen to stem from the pattern of liaison between statutory and voluntary action that is being attempted in the Borough as a whole. But they also reflect the more local class structure of Hope Green itself: the scheme is representative of many in that its "helpers" and "clients", although they are neighbours, belong to distinct social groups.

At the time of our survey, the Borough of Camden Social Services Department was making two broad attempts to promote neighbourhood care: there was a system of individual volunteers and good neighbours working directly with the department's area offices, and a network of supportive links with independent local voluntary projects. The volunteers and good neighbours involved in providing the first type of service – and who are definitely a semi-informal extension of the statutory system – can be distinguished from each other in several important ways. Both may well end up giving the same kind of help: virtually anything that will enable clients to "cope in their own homes". But the good neighbours live near the people they help and are paid a token sum for their assistance (and are required to report to the Area Office about the condition and circumstances of those they help). They are recruited fairly directly, either because they have approached the department themselves or because they have been recommended by an existing good neighbour or a social worker involved in a particular case, and their work is closely supervised by the department's organisers, who consider that the token payment not only ensures reliability and accountability in good neighbours, but also allows an effective monitoring of need via their reports. Prospective good neighbours are carefully vetted by the organisers, and great care is taken to match them with appropriate clients. Nevertheless, the good neighbours are seen as being most likely to be involved with a person living nearby or with a specific small area within which they are willing to be "on call" for emergencies. Their success or failure tends to be evaluated in terms of the lasting relationships formed with those they help, rather than in terms of the quantity of services delivered. By contrast, the volunteers have a less localised, more task-oriented and, in some ways, more professional approach.

The second type of service – the support for the neighbourhood care efforts of churches, voluntary organisations, tenants' and residents' associations and so on – involves the Department's organisers in co-ordinating the activities of different groups, offering advice and moral backing, discussing questions of policy and, to some extent, channeling referrals in suitable directions. The Department felt that a serious problem for this type of service was how to impose a measure of accountability on the various local groups.

Ironically, perhaps, the first problem facing Camden residents who might wish to launch an independent Good Neighbour Scheme – such as the founders of the Hope Green scheme – is to find room for their activities within this elaborate pattern of Social Services-based activities. The Area

Office organisers are themselves constantly on the lookout for new good neighbours and volunteers, and thus seem to cream off the most willing and suitable candidates, especially in working-class areas. So any new independent scheme has to compete. Since Camden is an authority in which councillors and senior officials are both committed to encouraging voluntary and community organisations, the competitiveness is at least relatively muted. But several of the scheme's more active members were acutely sensitive to the actual or presumed encroachment of the statutory services on the field of voluntary action. We must, however, record that several of the officials and local politicians we spoke to expressed anxiety about the tendency they saw among voluntary neighbourhood care projects to drift – even to throw themselves – into the arms of the state. The Council's good neighbour service had in fact begun as a voluntary project; the token payments had been introduced as a recruiting device – but the service had then got into financial difficulties and, in the end, could only be kept going by becoming "official". There is certainly no sense of rivalry, let alone hostility, on either side. The Hope Green Good Neighbours were concerned to state that they felt the situation was of mutual advantage – even if, for them, the advantage was little more than an official recognition that, provided their scheme worked, it would be cheaper than the Council's own service and "substantially cheaper" than the use of professionals. Apart from a generalised goodwill, in fact, the local authority had no explicit policy towards highly-localised schemes such as Hope Green. The working relationship between the statutory and voluntary systems was, in practice, left almost entirely to the discretion of the local patch social worker; as she put it, "basically it is my decision how far to go with the scheme". As it happened, she was keen to do what she could to help – but without "mothering" the scheme. For their part, the scheme organisers were eager to work closely with the statutory services: "they keep it all together", one said, and "it could collapse if we were completely on our own". Their aim was involvement without subservience. Yet, even on such an apparently positive basis, the problems of co-existence were acute.

At the time of our study, the scheme had existed for four years. Hope Green is an area of substantial older housing interspersed with patches of post-war council development. Although some of the older houses have decayed, there has been a good deal of careful preservation and "gentrification" in recent years. Accordingly, the population displays a wide social mixture. Members of the scheme were quite frank about the extent to which it had begun as a middle-class effort to help "less fortunate" people in the neighbourhood. Four years later, little had changed; not one of the 24 active helpers could realistically be described as anything but middle-class. And, since many of the younger people who had joined at the start had subsequently dropped out, the surviving members were not only firmly middle-class but also predominantly middle-aged; all but five were over 40. The scheme had been initiated by the SSD Area Office after difficulty had been experienced in Hope Green in recruiting good neighbours for the Department's own (paid) service. Not only had there been considerable enthusiasm for a voluntary scheme among the middle-class residents but, from the outset, some of the most active members had laid great stress on the distinction between voluntary and paid work; we were told several times that *not* being paid was one of the essential features of the scheme. Conversely, it was well understood that the success of the scheme therefore depended entirely upon the moral commitment of its members. But to transform enthusiasm into moral commitment had proved difficult. The problem was not so much the type of care that the scheme was providing; the general feeling amongst clients, the relevant statutory staff and those residents who knew anything about the scheme was that, *as far as it went,* the scheme had given Hope Green "a very friendly feeling" and that, precisely because the helpers *did* feel a commitment, many of their clients "would have been in a mess" without them. The problem was, in fact, that the scheme had shrunk in size since it began.

The original intention had been to provide three main types of help: visiting, transport and odd jobs. It was planned that two organisers should be appointed to co-ordinate each of these tasks but, by the time of our study, it was proving difficult to find and keep even one organiser for each field. In effect, the survival of the scheme had come to depend on the commitment of a single central person; it was widely agreed that, if she dropped out, the scheme would probably collapse altogether. Similarly, it had been part of the original plan to provide help for single-parent families and to organise child-minding and baby-sitting in cases of emergency, but in fact no-one had been found able and willing to take on such work. Furthermore, the scheme had never really succeeded in meeting local needs for transport on a regular basis; by the time of our visit, the local social worker rarely referred requests for transport to the scheme because she knew that they would either not be met or would mean even more work for the key organiser – perhaps the last straw. Those involved in the scheme were for the most part well aware of the difficulties and disappointments. They were by no means demoralised, or even reluctant to carry on; after four years, those who were still with the scheme had developed an involvement that made them well able to survive such setbacks. But they did often lament the fact that their present situation – one of relative isolation within the Hope Green community – fell far short of their original expectations. We discerned three aspects of this isolation. The hoped-for relationship between helpers and helped had simply failed to develop; visiting had not grown into friendship. The scheme had failed to widen its base to include working-class (or, as it was put, "less educated") helpers; there had once been two of them, but both had dropped out. And most widely cited was the failure of the scheme to expand: at the start there had been "a group who knew each other well" –

in particular, two men who "knew everyone locally and held the scheme together" – but now the scheme was felt to need "people to have enthusiasm . . . people can't go on pushing if they feel their efforts are going to fall through". A recent letter-box recruitment drive had had a "totally nil" response, and a leafletting of residents had "achieved nothing"; both were seen as evidence that "we just don't seem to be putting down any roots here". Since, as far as the organisers were concerned, one of the scheme's ideals had been to encourage the sort of neighbourly caring that "can function without organisation and has a real prop in community involvement", such perceived rootlessness after four years might have been expected to be much more discouraging for participants than we actually found it to be.

The truth seems to be that, although the Hope Green Scheme had failed to generate community involvement or to overcome its initial lack of an organic base in the life of the neighbourhood, the work it did do was being done effectively and was manifestly worthwhile. Emphasis had shifted, subtly but unmistakably, from neighbourliness to neighbourhood care – and, in that respect, the members of the scheme felt that they were doing well. Even though most helpers saw "isolation" as a major problem of contemporary society, and stressed their personal need to feel part of their local community, they were optimistic about the future of the scheme. Perhaps the members' optimism was a result of the fact that, although many of them asserted the scheme's value in "making the neighbourhood a more neighbourly place to live in", the single most important reason they gave for belonging to the scheme was simply the opportunity of "doing things for others". Although our interviews with the ordinary residents of Hope Green confirmed the scheme's "isolation" – for example, although 41 per cent of residents had heard of the scheme, only 5 per cent had any idea of what it did or how well – our interviews with the scheme's clients confirmed that the handful of active helpers were indeed doing a great deal for others in the neighbourhood.

The information we gathered about the scheme's clients did, in fact, confirm our general view of its problems and achievements – and also pointed towards the reasons for those successes and failures. Those helped by the members of the Hope Green Good Neighbour Scheme are almost all old and working-class. Most of the help consists of visiting, keeping the statutory services informed of the condition and needs of the clients, providing occasional transport, or doing "one-off" light chores. This pattern, according to one organiser, was "not intentional but the way it has worked out"; but the way it has worked out does again seem to be connected with the distinctive relationship between the scheme and its local environment on the one hand and the statutory authorities on the other. Almost all the "referrals" are brought to the scheme by the Social Services Department. The presence in Hope Green of a large new block of old people's flats also makes the elderly an obvious "target" for both the Social Services Department and the scheme. It was very clearly the needs of the elderly that the members of the scheme had had in mind when they spoke of what needed "doing for others". At the same time, the social and generation gap between helpers and the helped meant that even the most appreciative clients (and many were) viewed what was done for them as a "service" provided by "kind people" who "wanted to help others" – something that in their minds was quite distinct from relationships with friends and neighbours. For their part, many of the helpers spoke of the "difficulty of getting across" to those they helped. A less obvious, but perhaps more significant indicator of the nature of the relationship was, we noticed, the kind of "psychological means test" that helpers regularly applied to the helped – a test quite common in service relationships, but wholly untypical of relationships between friends. More or less explicitly, members of the scheme constantly assessed the extent to which their clients really deserved their help. Sometimes this was a straightforward financial appraisal: "she could perfectly well afford a taxi". But more often it was the feeling that the person concerned was making "unreasonable demands", in the sense of being insufficiently feeble or isolated enough to claim the attention of the scheme; one helper abruptly stopped taking out a man in his wheelchair when she discovered he had a daughter in the neighbourhood. Generally speaking, the members of the scheme thought it quite reasonable to apply an instinctive "calculus of need" to the people they were invited to help. On the one hand, this meant that their efforts were concentrated where they were most needed – a very sensible economy. But, on the other hand, it meant that their actions were more immediately recognisable as a social service than as any sort of neighbourliness or friendship.

The key to this situation is, in our view, the relationship between the Hope Green Scheme and the local Social Services. That relationship is in itself ambiguous, but it does dominate everything that the scheme does and is; including the fact that it is *not* an organic part of the everyday life of Hope Green. As far as the members and organisers of the scheme are concerned, their close relationship with the statutory services is not simply desirable but vital – a feeling that clearly stems not only from their lack of contact with the local community but also from the fact that, in the early years of the scheme, the statutory services were very supportive. Ironically, this very closeness is now seen as a disadvantage by many of the statutory staff associated with the scheme. In encouraging the scheme initially, the Area Office apparently hoped to plant a seed of self-help in the community that would grow into a largely independent (albeit effectively monitored) venture. In practice, the organisers of the scheme have tended to compensate for their lack of a community base by clinging to the official connection. At the time of our survey, most of the relevant statutory staff felt that they should gently manoeuvre the scheme into a greater autonomy and a closer connection with other community organisations: "they've tended to look for support too much and we've tended to give too much". From an official point of view, the value of schemes such as Hope Green is clearly related to their ability to provide reliable and effective care without the constant input of expensive professional support. For their part, the organisers and activists within the scheme were sceptical about the feasibility of such independence – or, as one official claimed, simply "frightened" of it. Certainly, given their lack of alternative resources and personnel, the organisers of the scheme do attach great value to the knowledge and training of the professionals and to the fact that they are readily available in cases of difficulties. And they "do not like the idea of being cut off" from that kind of support when no alternative support is at hand from the community.

When we visited Hope Green, the immediate focus of all these concerns was a proposal that the Good Neighbours Scheme should apply for a council grant to pay for renting space in a local "Advice Shop", for the telephone bill and for other incidental expenses. Extensive discussion had led to the official verdict that "the scheme can't grow any more without autonomy" and an interweaving of its activities with those of other voluntary groups in the neighbourhood. The Area Office accordingly encouraged the organisers of the scheme to apply for a small grant, as a way of manoeuvring them towards autonomy. With considerable reluctance, the organisers had made the application and received the grant. Their reluctance was a conscious response not only to their past experience of official support for the scheme, but also to their lack of community involvement. The main organiser felt that "autonomy" could well turn out to mean that, in place of a "regular and informal rapport" with the Social Services – which often meant that, whenever the demands on the scheme's helpers became unmanageable, the load was readily taken over – they would find themselves in a vacuum in which "we would simply be told to get on with it". Every member of the scheme had "mixed feelings" about the grant, and several were said to be "glad we only applied for the grant for six months". Yet, at the same time as they were voicing fears about the loss of their close contact with the statutory services, members of the scheme – including the hard-pressed organisers – expressed similar doubts about the suggestion to appoint a part-time paid organiser, largely because they thought this might tie them too closely to those very same services: "It would mean a change to being a branch of the statutory services"; "the scheme would lose its voluntary aspect, lose out on the feeling of it being local help, we should just be one more cog in a wheel"; "it would make us into something quite different – the essence of what we do is that we are voluntary and unpaid".

These and other questions, such as the case for and against charging clients for transport, were live issues within the scheme when we studied it. Then, as earlier – and later – its existence depended upon constant change and adaptation. It was too soon to say whether the hesitant move towards autonomy would reduce the scheme's dependence on the statutory services and strengthen its connections with the local community, or whether it would isolate it doubly. It was much too soon to say whether, beyond the general feeling that "it would be better to have a paid organiser than to let the scheme collapse altogether", there was the real possibility of a more expansive future. But the specific answers to such questions do not really matter in this context. We are more concerned to point out that the predicament of the Hope Green Good Neighbour Scheme demonstrates not only how delicate is the balance that needs to be struck between schemes and the statutory services, as well as between schemes and their community, but also how ambiguous is the concept of success where such schemes are concerned. A scheme that fails to encourage neighbourliness can nevertheless do a great deal of good to others.

### 6 Riverside Good Neighbour Service

The Riverside Good Neighbour Service has what so many schemes say they need: a full-time paid organiser. A large scheme operating in a "difficult" London borough, it is widely regarded as successful – and many of those associated with it will readily tell you that the full-time organiser has played a major part in that success. The service was set up in 1965 by the old District Nursing Association as a means of continuing to exploit that Association's assets after responsibility for home nursing had, under local government reorganisation, passed to the statutory authorities. Thereafter, the service became an independent project, a registered charity loosely associated with the borough's Voluntary Services Council. Initially independent financially, the service was later granted Urban Aid to enable expansion, but investment income, voluntary contributions and the members' own fundraising still account for more than half the total income. The service is managed by a small executive committee, about half of whose members are active "field" volunteers. At the time of our study, the mayor of the borough was President. The service has a well-staffed and business-like office in a building that also accommodates the VSC, a Settlement, and a variety of other voluntary service projects. The area for which the service is responsible under the terms of its constitution had, at the last census, a population of 93,511, just under 17 per cent of whom were of pensionable age. Clearly, a scheme that operates on this scale cannot base its work on the kind of close-knit teams that are so important to smaller projects. In contrast to the situation in, say, Pitside or Hope Green, in fact, the majority of the helpers we spoke to in Riverside did not know one another. The usual pattern of work is for individual volunteers to help specific clients who live near them; the executive provides efficient co-ordination and considerable moral support, but there is relatively little of the concern to develop relationships *among* the helpers that is so marked in the Reaching Good

94

Neighbours or the Greenwich Task Force project. There is an annual party for all helpers that provides a welcome "opportunity to discuss matters of mutual concern", and numerous meetings and collective fund-raising projects are also organised, but one of the few reservations that helpers had about the GNS was that they tended to be isolated with the people they helped rather than part of a larger group. Against that, however, we must point out that this was one of the very few schemes we examined whose members commonly described it as "100 per cent successful".

In the year preceding our study, the Riverside GNS dealt with 791 requests for help. The organiser was particularly pleased with the fact that 49 per cent of these "came about non-officially", either as a result of direct approaches by friends, relatives, neighbours or the prospective clients themselves, or were generated by the GNS helpers. For her, a significant indication of the progress of the GNS was that "more and more people were contacting us direct about their needs and those of their family and friends . . . help locally should not have to depend on social workers finding out there is a crisis". Of the remaining referrals, 30 per cent had come from Social Services and a further 17 per cent from local hospitals, clinics, health visitors, doctors and nurses. Roughly 90 per cent of the requests (704) were for short-term help; the various publications of the GNS clearly show that this is the type of assistance – either "one-off" or over a limited time-span— that the service's helpers are best able to provide. The variety of such help is, however, wider than most schemes can manage: not simply the usual transport, escorting, shopping and collecting, emergency cooking and washing, child-minding and sitting with the lonely, but also home decorating and repairs, carpentry and electrical work, gardening, home hairdressing, pet-minding, correspondence and help with languages. The GNS has the usual difficulties with requests for transport – which account for about 27 per cent of the total – even though drivers are offered a mileage allowance (few of them, in fact, accept it). And requests for long-term commitment to visiting or befriending are "always subject to a waiting list". The organiser has sometimes been able to meet calls for more sustained or intensive assistance by organising a rota of helpers in order to spread the load; one bed-bound old woman, for example, was provided with meals and a late-night drink at weekends for a period of many months – from the time of referral until she was admitted to a residential home, in fact. But the capacity of the GNS to provide that kind of help is limited: in the year prior to our visit, of the 87 requests that called for an open-ended or long-term commitment by a volunteer to a client on a one-to-one basis, the majority "turned out to be non-starters for various reasons". Thirty-four of these long-term requests were, in fact, met, but the GNS is nevertheless uneasily aware that, most of the time, there are quite a number of people in Riverside who badly need friendship and company that it is beyond the service's resources to provide. Here again, the contrast with Pitside is striking. All

95

the organising ability and enthusiasm in the world – and the Riverside GNS has been lucky in attracting a great deal of both – cannot generate the kind of mutual involvement between neighbours that develops over the years in small, well-defined communities where families and work-groups have hardly changed for generations. The organiser insists that she "cannot urge too often the need for local residents to spare time for their elderly or handicapped neighbours". But most of the helpers we interviewed seemed to find Riverside a very lonely place where contact between neighbours is fleeting, and quite as likely to be based on mistrust as on goodwill. One helper described the work she did for the GNS as the kind of thing that "would be done normally in a village; here you wouldn't know your neighbours; once you close your front door you're isolated . . . I've lived here forty years". And another said, more bluntly, "round here it's simply appalling . . . people are very unfriendly". In a place such as Riverside, any attempt to root care in neighbourliness is perhaps Utopian; but the GNS has at least demonstrated over the years that modest resources sensibly used can significantly increase the amount of help local people give one another and the extent to which people in need of care can receive it in their own homes.

From that point of view, one impressive aspect of the Riverside scheme is the fact that despite withdrawals, the number of its volunteers and helpers increases steadily year by year. By 1977 the service had recruited between 140 and 150 helpers (36 having been recruited in the previous twelve months to replace the 20 who had dropped out during the same period). By 1980, the total had reached 200. The organiser devotes much time and energy to recruitment, and most of the helpers seem to have joined as a direct result of her efforts. Interestingly, most of the "drop-outs" appear to have been the result of such unavoidable factors as pregnancy, illness or leaving the district, rather than a loss of interest. The organiser devotes almost as much energy to looking after her helpers as she does to meeting the needs of the service's clients; to judge from the feelings of usefulness and success reported by the helpers themselves, her effort clearly pays off. Indeed, when some helpers were asked why they gave the help they did, they replied simply that they did it for the organiser: "She's so active". The drawback to that kind of commitment was, of course, the fact that numerous helpers were obviously highly dependent on the organiser for support and advice; they had, for example, little idea of how the service related to other agencies and activities in Riverside, or of how to cope with problems other than those specifically assigned to them. They seemed to need to shelter behind authority and expertise: "If you can say the organiser sent you, people don't think you're being nosy"; "If I'm given a job by the organiser I wouldn't worry about it, but most of them are things I wouldn't do on my own". When helpers were asked what they would do if an unexpected problem arose with their clients, a common answer was "I'd ask the organiser". It was possible to see how, with a little less care, the service could well have turned into an excessively centralised structure with very few horizontal connections at the lower levels. It was perhaps only the measures taken to bring helpers together from time to time, to organise events at which helpers and clients could meet (such as Christmas Day together at the GNS headquarters for those who would otherwise have been on their own) and to sustain a flow of information by means of newsletters, circulars and reports, that prevented the development of such over-centralisation.

That danger was, however, offset by the manifestly high morale of the helpers, who generally seemed to feel that they were successful in providing help where it was needed. The helpers range in age from 18 to over 70 and come from very diverse social backgrounds. In this respect, it is perhaps an advantage that they rarely meet and mix as a group: the interpersonal tensions so evident at Pitside, and in a rather different way at Hope Green, were noticeably absent from the Riverside GNS. For the most part, helpers see the project quite straightforwardly as "filling a gap which the Social Services don't cover" – which is also the organiser's view of things. There is no question of the GNS also being a venture in neighbourliness for the helpers. The size and diversity of the pool of helpers means that when a need is reported to the organiser, she can usually match the prospective client to an appropriate helper in a carefully-considered way; she can also be quite tough-minded about refusing to take on cases she judges unsuitable for the GNS and better handled by other agencies. All this has a good deal to do with the satisfaction most helpers seem to derive from the work they do; the fact that the office has unusually detailed information about what they are able and willing to do means that they are usually given a task they can perform well. Some helpers, for example, have over the years become virtual specialists in dealing with certain kinds of tasks or certain types of client: one had spent ten years with the GNS "mostly shopping", another had often helped by minding pets – "I've had hundreds of cats" – and yet another, who considered herself incapable of communicating with the elderly, had in fact visited and talked to many old people in the course of redecorating their homes – work she was good at, and liked doing. A fourth, whose husband had been confined to a wheelchair after an accident, simply took other chair-bound people on outings. But we are not suggesting that this kind of specialisation is essential. Some of the most satisfied helpers in the Riverside GNS were those who did a bit of everything: "My main thing is with elderly people. We're taking a family down to Brighton. I visit four old people regularly. I do somebody's washing and a bit of gardening for someone else. Another one I get fish and chips for on a Saturday. I just feel we're helping people and I enjoy it, it's as simple as that. It's the satisfaction of seeing my old people's faces – you should see them." But this particular helper did add "I suppose I'm lucky" – and it does seem that, for many, giving help to others is only possible within a carefully-structured and circumscribed context. And that is something that a strong, centrally co-ordinated scheme such as the Riverside GNS does allow.

# V
# National Agencies and Policies

In chapter 3 we pointed out that relations with external statutory and voluntary organisations can be a major problem for Good Neighbour Schemes. We also noted that there seemed to be great variations between the policies and attitudes of these organisations from county to county. In this chapter we shall attempt to put those findings in a national context.

In addition to the statutory welfare services, many 'voluntary sector' organisations have become closely associated with the promotion of neighbourhood care in recent years. Many of them are, indeed, directly involved in working with Good Neighbour Schemes. In this chapter we shall therefore give short descriptions of the objectives of some of these organisations at national level, based on information provided by the organisations themselves. Whenever possible, we shall quote directly from the statements the organisations sent us; in a few cases, however, we have summarised their published literature. We are presenting this material in order to provide an overview of the environment for Good Neighbouring that is created by the current concern of these national agencies with organised neighbourhood care.

The emphasis on giving care in a neighbourhood context, using local residents themselves as care-givers, can be seen as a positive move away from the traditionally more individualistic voluntary service approach, where a centralized agency matches care-givers and the cared-for on a person-to-person basis. The latter system has often been criticised for its tendency to isolate volunteers and their clients: volunteers may lack the support of a group of people involved in the same situation; and they may not live in the same area as their client, with a consequent lack of the shared experiences of a locality. A more *mutual* provision of care, the encouragement of friendships and positive "neighbourliness", within a network of helpers and helped is the basis of the new approach to neighbourhood care. Those who give voluntary help are increasingly stressing not only the necessity of confronting the problems of accountability, dependence and control, but also the desirability of "caring for the care-givers" by generating "community" and sociability. Task Force, for instance, seeks to initiate neighbourhood care schemes that have the declared aim of developing a local autonomy that will eventually render the scheme's own participation unnecessary; and Age Concern has attempted to encourage reciprocity between helpers and helped through its Link schemes. Such thoroughgoing changes in social policy clearly offer an exciting challenge to the national organisations mentioned here. Above all, they present new opportunities for revolutionising the provision of voluntary neighbourhood care – a provision that those organisations have shaped so decisively in the past. Also important is the rapid growth, particularly during the last decade, of voluntary groups and initiatives that, in their aims and methods, represent "alternatives" to the approach of the "mainstream" voluntary sector. Here, the emphasis is more directly on promoting collective self-help among those in need of care and support or among those living in a particular locality (or both), than on help provided by an "outside" agency. Although some of these organisations do have a national structure, it is usually of a loose and accountable kind; the overall stress is on the need for local groups of people to retain independence and control. Also, there is often an explicit concern with campaigning, with confronting the power of existing bureaucracies and vested interests, and with challenging the "official" definitions of people and their needs. But this need not, and does not, diminish the importance of social activities, personal friendships or the provision of care – which may not be part of an organised system of care-giving, but may instead develop informally from the contacts and networks built up through other activities.

Given this report's chief concern, we have included several projects and organisations providing neighbourhood care that seem to fall into this "alternative" category because of their structure and/or policies. Some, for example, are the product of spontaneous local initiative: a Pensioners' Action Group, or those Tenants' and Residents' Associations and Community Associations whose "social" aspect provides a basis for care-giving in their locality. The growth in "alternative" projects since the 1970s seems likely to continue. These new networks of people already serve an extraordinarily wide range of needs, causes and interests: for example, the gay, black and women's movements, housing groups, amenity and environmental projects, local peoples' aid centres, and organisations such as Gingerbread. Even within the most strict definition of care-giving, the strategies of some of these voluntary associations can be regarded as embodying crucial elements of the recent general trends we have outlined above. For example, the Multiple Sclerosis Society, founded in 1953, emphasises care and support of and by its members, and promotes "the formation of branches and local groups all over the United Kingdom to arrange mutual help and comradeship and to bring interest and hope into the lives of MS patients". Recognition of the value of mutuality, collective self-support, independence from "external" control and a localised social base is, of course, not new: indeed, it is part of the democratic tendency that has characterised the development of popular movements and associations ever since the last century.

There are, of course, significant differences between these groups and organisations. By no means all of them share the same set of values, and there is considerable variation in the level of neighbourhood organisation and care-giving they encourage. We simply wish to stress that groups with an explicit label of "neighbourhood care" or "good neighbouring", or who include neighbourhood care among their stated aims, are not the *only* providers of informal care within our society. In addition, this general movement towards community involvement and special causes has strongly influenced not only the way in which care is provided but also the way in which neighbourhood care itself is organised. And, finally, the issues raised by the policies of these groups – and their attendant questions of social composition, organisational structure, success, hierarchies, control, self reliance and interpersonal relations – are inherent in the provision of neighbourhood care of any kind and from any source – although in practice they are often suppressed or ignored rather than openly confronted.

This chapter is concerned with the policies, and allied trends, that affect the provision of neighbourhood care as a framework for Good Neighbouring. We hope that the various approaches and possibilities outlined above will provide a useful basis for considering the necessarily brief accounts of policy that follow, and will aid the reader's appraisal of the nature, effects and implications of different policies for neighbourhood care. Our intention is not to urge one particular position, but describe what is actually happening in the policy field at a national level. It is a fundamental tenet of Good Neighbouring that people and organisations should be left to decide what is appropriate and effective for them.

## 1 Task Force

Task Force is a London-based organisation with a staff of 60 working to improve the conditions of the elderly. To this end it supports groups of pensioners who meet to overcome common problems, and deploys volunteers to visit and give practical aid to housebound pensioners.

Over the past 5 years Task Force has been working to develop or support neighbourhood care schemes in many London boroughs both inside and outside the inner city. It views them as opportunities for local people to take control of the provision of voluntary service, rather than as external agencies providing charity. In addition to providing a "more relevant and immediate service", it has found that the divisions between helpers and helped are often broken down. Indeed, pensioners, who are otherwise looked upon as users of social services, play a major role in the success of such schemes.

Task Force sees the self-determination of neighbourhood schemes as a key factor in their long-term success. This may result in the objectives of the neighbourhood care scheme being at variance with Task Force policy. It is Task Force policy, for example, not to use volunteers to carry out the work of home helps etc, though a Good Neighbour Scheme may see it as part of their job to shop or do housework for pensioners. In such instances of conflicting policies, the Task Force worker will not impose his/her view on the group but explain the background and reasons for Task Force policy.

Task Force hopes that Good Neighbour Schemes, though self-run, will not become too formal or structured in their operation. Through community development the aim is to develop a level of good neighbour-liness in an area, without necessarily creating an organisation, committee or formal group. This obviously takes time, and workers may spend 2 years developing one scheme as a major part of their work.

While neighbourhood care has much to commend it in its own right, it would, in the view of Task Force, "be naive to ignore its relationship to other services provided by both statutory and voluntary agencies". Good Neighbour Schemes, according to Task Force, should not – indeed, cannot – provide the degree of casework support available from a Social Worker: "The role of formal caring and neighbourhood care schemes are clearly different. Far from being interchangeable, the two sectors complement each other. A framework of adequate statutory services is the only context in which neighbourhood care can flourish".

Task Force is accordingly "extremely concerned by the view of some local authorities who look upon Good Neighbour Schemes as an alternative to the services which they are cutting". Community care of this kind diminishes during times of economic recession rather than increasing to compensate for cuts in statutory services. This is inevitable as more working people are forced to consider their own hardships as a priority.

*Contact address:*
Chris Long
Development Worker
Task Force
Hereditable House
28/29 Dover Street
London W1


## 2   The British Association of Social Workers

The British Association of Social Workers believes that general acceptance of the concept of the Caring Community, as well as mobilisation of community resources, are both essential to the development of a proper standard of care within the community. There are continuing roles for voluntary organisations and volunteers in the Social Services field as:

1   Pioneers: developing specialist facilities before they have been adequately identified to the extent where public services are prepared to provide money, and;

102

2   Providing parallel services: this allows clients some choice in the source of help and encourages more work in depth with people with particular problems.

In many discussions about neighbourhood care, it is necessary to make the distinction between voluntary organisations which may employ paid social work staff and those using volunteers who may or may not have social work qualifications. The Association's concern to explore the appropriate contributions of the professional social worker and the individual volunteer resulted in a research project being commissioned. The research, undertaken by Anthea Holme and Joan Maizels, has been published by Allen and Unwin under the title *Social Workers and Volunteers;* it is intended to provide information on:—

a)  the extent to which social workers make use of volunteers and the type of task undertaken by the latter,
b)  how social workers view the contribution made by the volunteer worker, and;
c)  to identify and examine some of the factors accounting for the use by social workers of volunteer helpers.

In its comments on the Home Office consultative document *The Government and the Voluntary Sector*, the Association stated that a long-term strategy needs to be developed at national, regional and local level. Such a strategy should be directed at clarifying the relationship between statutory and voluntary sectors, thus allowing a more planned approach to the allocation of resources in the "who does what?" debate. To this end, the Association welcomes the proposal to strengthen the Voluntary Services Unit in the Home Office in an attempt to provide a more effective link between Government and the people.

The Association is in frequent contact with associations representing voluntary organisations and the volunteer dimension, including The Volunteer Centre. The purpose of such contacts is to ensure that professional social workers are informed about, and encouraged to reflect on, programmes and new initiatives relating to a range of voluntary activities.

*Contact address:*
John Cypher
Assistant General Secretary
British Association of Social Workers
16 Kent Street
Birmingham B5 6RD.

## 3   WRVS Good Companions Scheme

The WRVS Good Companions Scheme was started in 1971. The WRVS had been approached by the Secretary of State at the DHSS about the need of certain classes of housebound people for more help than is provided by visiting schemes, which are primarily concerned with alleviating loneliness. There was a growing number of people who, owing to age, disablement or other misfortune, were finding it difficult to continue to live happily and safely in their own homes and who needed some help to encourage them to remain independent.

On the assumption that the help required would be of the sort which in the ordinary way would be provided by a near relative, Good Companions was started as a one-to-one service, with the Good Companion being willing to give whatever assistance was required, according to the needs of the person being helped. The Good Companion service is organised on a local or district basis, with an Organiser in charge of each scheme, thus ensuring continuity. An initial visit is made by the Organiser to assess the needs of the person referred for help, and where it is considered desirable, more than one Good Companion will be allocated to a case.

Although Good Companions is a WRVS-run service, each scheme works closely with the local authority Social Services Department, and help is requested from the Home Help and Meals on Wheels Services, the Health Visitors, Social Workers, etc as required.

The Good Companion scheme is not limited to helping the elderly, and more and more requests are being received for help with other age groups: stroke victims; widows who, because of their bereavement, are tending to become withdrawn; people coming out of hospital who require short-term help; young wives with babies who have moved to a strange town because of their husband's work; the single person tied by a dependent relative; befriending people through a period of depression; and so on.

All helpers in the scheme are unpaid volunteers. We are assisted in many instances by other voluntary bodies such as the Women's Institute, the Salvation Army, Church groups, etc.

Financial support to cover the Good Companions' travelling expenses can be received from County Councils, Area Health Authorities or various other funding bodies. The cost to the Good Companion of bus fares or petrol is the major problem facing the schemes in most areas. This is particularly so where the "matching-up" of the person in need with a suitable Good Companion is vital and where frequent long journeys have to be made as a consequence. Regular visits on a continuing basis means a considerable outlay by the Good Companion, so before any new scheme is started WRVS has to be certain that the costs, however small, will be covered.

*Contact address:*
Sheila Hurwitz
Women's Royal Voluntary Service
17 Old Park Lane
London W1Y 4AJ.

## 4   Voluntary Services Unit (Home Office)

In discharging its responsibilities of giving support to (mainly national) voluntary organisations and also of co-ordinating government policy towards the voluntary sector, the Voluntary Services Unit is very mindful of the important part played by informal caring systems. It recognises and accepts that the primary system of care upon which the majority must depend in times of need is provided on an informal basis, and would welcome the development of new methods for strengthening such informal provision. In considering proposals for schemes, whether in the voluntary or the statutory sectors, on which its comment is invited, it takes particular note of the consequences or side effects insofar as they might have an effect upon the safety net of informal caring systems.

*Contact address:*
J C Hindley
Voluntary Services Unit
Home Office
Queen Anne's Gate
London SW1H 9AT.

## 5   Help the Aged

Help the Aged launched a Good Neighbour Scheme some years ago to prevent some frightening and needless deaths among old people who are living alone. This scheme caught the imagination of people everywhere, and already a chain of helpers are unofficially keeping an eye on older neighbours living nearby.

Old people living alone, especially if they have no telephone to call for help, can so easily become ill without anyone knowing; and being ill alone, even for a few hours, can be a frightening experience. Help the Aged is asking that, wherever an old person is known to be living alone, the immediate neighbours should have some rota for watching for signs that all is well. A person living opposite can watch for the curtains being drawn back in the morning; if the house is semi-detached or terraced, sounds can be listened for at certain times of the day; a further point to watch for can be the light going on in the evening. Any regular shopping habits should be noted and if a person is not seen at the usual time, an excuse to call can be thought of. Even the most independent old person will not resent intrusion if he is ill and in need of help.

If the elderly neighbour is quite happy to have people around keeping an eye on him then a more obvious call for help signal can be arranged such as a card in the window or some similar device. If this person is on the 'phone, it is a good idea to have a card with a few numbers in large print near the 'phone so that help can be called quickly. Also, the 'phone should be placed on a low table in case of a fall; lives have been saved by a person pulling himself along the floor to a telephone. In any case, by dialling 100 they can contact the operator, who will get help. However, even with such safety measures as a telephone and special help signals, the normal signs of life should be watched for.

Those willing to take such organisation further should appeal for a person in every road to be responsible for finding where old people live and then asking those living near to help. The local churches, local papers or local radio stations will give help with this. People want to help but are so afraid of seeming nosy or interfering. In the experience of Help the Aged, the elderly welcome an interest being taken in them – even the independent ones. It should also be remembered that elderly people, provided they are fit, could make some of the best street wardens. They know the habits of their neighbours and are quick to spot any change in routine.

This can bring much happiness to an area. Gradually people get to know each other better, and the younger ones welcome the increased friendship with older people which so many miss in these days when families are frequently spread around the country; concern for others can unite a road.

We urge that everyone should remember that the Social Services are always there to help if you are worried about an elderly neighbour. A telephone call will meet with a quick and sympathetic response. If general health is a problem, contact your health visitor at the local clinic. Again you will receive advice and help. No one need feel that he has taken on too much responsibility. There are excellent support services and their telephone numbers are in every local directory. It might be a good idea to look up these numbers now and have them ready in case of emergency.

You may wish to run your own Good Neighbour Scheme quite independently; then we would say "Good luck, and go ahead". However, Help the Aged would be interested to hear of people's efforts to run such schemes, even if only one old person was being looked after in this way, and it might be of interest to others to hear of any new ideas you may have.

*Contact address:*
Good Neighbours, Help the Aged
32 Dover Street
London W1A 2AP.


## 6   Age Concern

For many years Age Concern has set out to promote the development of neighbourhood care. It is implicit in many of its policies, and much of the work being carried out by some 1300 local groups within the Age Concern movement could be described in this way. The process can be identified with the majority of its widely-accepted priorities and many of its innovative programmes, whether they are concerned with early warning systems, *ad hoc* arrangements or sustained inter-personal support networks.

However, because every Age Concern group is autonomous and takes independent decisions about the range and nature of the services it will promote, and the settings in which they will be offered, it is probably unlikely that the movement as a whole could arrive at a definition of the exact nature of neighbourhood care that would command universal acceptance and would be capable of application in widely different local circumstances. Perhaps the nearest to a consensus might be a general agreement that there is an inherent mutuality within the process by which givers and receivers of care can sense common social objectives and physical proximity that binds them together.

Age Concern's belief in the need to encourage neighbourhood care systems can be identified with two major convictions. Firstly, the belief that even the resources of statutory services and the traditional voluntary sector in combination are insufficient to provide an adequate response to the diversity of old people's needs. Secondly, as a more positive expression of the benefit of good neighbourly service, there is the belief that a sense of shared interest or common identity enhances the value of relationships. It actually makes it easier in practice to provide help on terms which are acceptable to those for whom it is designed, without much of the ambivalence that can often reduce the value of service offered through more formal structures or can lead to total rejection.

This concept of shared interest is regarded by Age Concern as having particular significance because it is more likely to stimulate reciprocal care systems, and because the expressions of care given through informal neighbourhood networks will be seen to have qualities of naturalness, relaxation and spontaneity that are likely to be missing from the more rigid framework of a professional relationship constrained by time and probably separated by social class and distance.

Closely linked to this belief is the view that, when help fails to take account of the recipients' need to maintain a personal sense of worth and dignity, the process may lead to unnecessary dependency.

Clearly, a sense of shared concern is not to be found universally, even within neighbourhoods; but Age Concern believes it can be fostered by bringing people together to take corporate decisions in their localities. As a result, it is attempting to develop the process of local consultation as a means of channelling views to decision-makers responsible for resource allocation within both local and central government.

This reflects a commitment to participation described in its manifesto on the place of the retired and elderly in modern society.

In an organisational context, numbers of local Age Concern groups are using the mechanism of street warden schemes, village representatives, and informal "pop-in" parlours or pensioners' clubs to combine the provision of service with the encouragement of individual participation, as well as to provide a means of discovering the nature of neighbourhood needs and aspirations by creating a sense of identity through which objectives can be agreed and caring relationships developed and nurtured.

107

*Contact address:*
Age Concern
Bernard Sunley House
60 Pitcairn Road
Mitcham
Surrey.


## 7   National Council for Voluntary Organisations

Several thousand national and local voluntary organisations are able to work together through the National Council for Voluntary Organisations. NCVO aims:

- to extend the involvement of voluntary organisations in responding to social issues,
- to be a resource centre for voluntary organisations,
- to protect the interests and independence of voluntary organisations.

NCVO works closely with local councils for voluntary service (CVS), rural community councils (RCC), and other voluntary groups. NCVO is particularly concerned to develop opportunities for individual involvement in local voluntary groups, believing that such involvement is increasingly important for the health and vitality of our society.

Good Neighbour projects involve people helping one another in the community. Run by volunteers committed to giving neighbourly help to the disabled, elderly, housebound and others in need, they provide many people with the opportunity to become directly involved in meeting human needs. As this directory indicates, Good Neighbour Schemes differ in many respects; some have paid staff to co-ordinate activities, while others are organised by volunteers; they can cover a whole area or just a few streets or blocks of flats.

Many of NCVO's affiliated organisations have been involved in promoting Good Neighbour projects and similar community care schemes – including, for example, Hastings, Harlow and Brighton Councils for Voluntary Service. Manchester CVS, in collaboration with the City of Manchester Social Services Department and Manchester Neighbourhood Care Groups, has produced a booklet *Neighbourhood Care Groups in Manchester;* the aim of this booklet is to inform more individuals and organisations about the services offered by such local groups, and to show their contribution in making community care a reality.

Similarly, this directory provides a wealth of examples of Good Neighbour and similar schemes. It will be instrumental both in stimulating voluntary action and in indicating the valuable contribution of the informal carers.

*Contact address:*
National Council for Voluntary Organisations
26 Bedford Square
London WC1B 3HU.


## 8   Royal Association for Disability and Rehabilitation

The Royal Association believes that one of the bedrocks of a caring community must be a desire to help one another; for, if we believe that there is always someone else who will provide for the needs of our neighbours, our whole system must be doomed.

Disabled people probably more than others need a helping hand and occasional assistance to live in the community and to assert their right to be part of it.

There is still twice as much voluntary help in this country as statutory, and much of this help is at neighbourhood level. RADAR believes that the wish to help others is increasing and that it is a trend which must be fostered and encouraged.

This directory, which gives examples of so many varied schemes at all levels in the community, will do much to encourage others to provide similar practical and valuable help.

*Contact address:*
Royal Association for Disability and Rehabilitation
25 Mortimer Street
London W1N 8AB.


## 9   The Volunteer Centre

The Volunteer Centre, the national advisory agency on volunteer and community involvement in the statutory and voluntary services, has neighbourhood care as a theme running through all its work. The Centre is especially interested in ways in which:

— neighbours, friends and family can be helped to give help informally.
— those helpers can be supported by other volunteers through such frameworks as neighbourhood care schemes.
— statutory and voluntary bodies can interlock with volunteer and informal help, as in, for example, social services "patch" systems and primary health care teams.

The Centre is looking at ways of helping the organisers of voluntary neighbourhood projects – whether they work in Fish schemes, community care projects, Good Neighbour Schemes or under any of the other titles in this directory. Where projects aim to reproduce or support informal care in small localities, there are at least two common problems. The first of these is sheer isolation. One of the ways in which the Centre is trying to counter this is through *Volunteers in the Neighbourhood*, a quarterly news-sheet for neighbourhood care organisers and the people who manage them. The news-sheet deals with practical problems – getting started, publicity, finance, training – as well as with the special needs of rural and inner city projects. It also gives short descriptions of projects and contacts for further information.

The second problem for organisers is that of acquiring appropriate skills. There is a steady flow of enquiries to The Volunteer Centre from people who, all over the UK, are independently working out how to tackle similar problems. Some of the advice we give has been condensed into publications such as *Limited Liability*, which looks at the advantage of different forms of organisation. A number of schemes are examined in detail in *A Case in Point*, a series of case studies describing a wide variety of projects.

Among other useful reading for people trying to set up a neighbourhood scheme is *Community Partnership: a community's perspective*, in which a community worker in a South London borough describes the problems of establishing a scheme to strengthen the network of informal care for old people with an alarm system manned by friends, relatives and volunteers. Community care organisers will understand the message that there *can* be a conflict of interests between community organisations, trades unions and social services departments, even when their over-riding goal is the well-being of the elderly – but that there can also be a happy outcome!

To be published in 1981 are *Neighbours' Eye Views*, in which people up and down the country describe how they see themselves and others as neighbours, good or bad, spontaneous or thoughtful, considerate or careless; and *What the Neighbours Say,* which takes the viewpoint of the neighbourhood worker, whether minister, community worker, health visitor or care organiser – it describes ways of getting to know and understand the frequently opaque and complex relations between neighbours, and some of the factors that encourage or prevent neighbourly action.

The Volunteer Centre is trying to change the attitudes of workers in the statutory services. It wants these workers to give more support and encouragement to the informal carers. They could do this simply by recognising their existence, also by making an effort to pass on relevant skills and knowledge, by making material resources available, and by trying to share the burden and cost (emotional, physical and financial) of caring. The Centre is helping to reshape the basic training of professionals, to show that the community is not simply a source of problems but a reservoir of skills, knowledge and talent. Many of these caring resources, the Centre argues, already exist and are used in the community without the help of professionals; but there is potential for a great deal more to be released, given the proper skills and knowledge among those workers who can help to release it.

The Volunteer Centre works mainly through publications and through giving general answers to specific enquiries. But are there other ways in which a national advisory agency can help organisers of neighbourhood projects? Conferences, courses, meetings, training programmes perhaps, at local or national level? We should like to hear more from organisers, and from those responsible for their work, about what is needed and what we can do about it.

If you have ideas, or need information, or would like the full publications list or details of the case study series, please write or 'phone.

*Contact address:*
The Volunteer Centre
29 Lower King's Road
Berkhamsted
Herts HP4 2AB
Telephone (04427) 73311.

## *10 Contact*

Contact is a way of helping people to channel their ability to care, beyond their own family, for elderly people living near them.

We provide a framework within which lies the core of an idea which people can take up and make their own – a simple act of friendship.

A contact group at its best can fulfil in some part the need of everyone to give and to feel valued – both older and younger members. At the same time it can meet a desperate need among the old, to whom loneliness is like a disease.

We know a great deal about loneliness in Contact. The elderly people in our groups – and their ages range from the late 70s upwards – live alone with limited, inadequate or no family support; they have difficulty, for reasons ranging from disability to lack of confidence, in getting out unaided and are, as a result, isolated and lonely; in fact, those who, with statutory and voluntary help, are trying to live on in their own homes. Social Workers and those in other caring professions throughout the country refer their clients to us for care within a Contact group.

It is a timeless idea which brings together a group of people spanning all ages, abilities, energy and preferences. By its very nature, the group allows people to put in as much as they are willing and able to do; but, at the same time, no-one will make them feel guilty if they stay within the minimum Contact commitment of one Sunday afternoon a month – about five hours.

A Contact volunteer offers companionship in the form of a monthly Sunday afternoon outing with the other members of the group to someone's home for tea. At least half of the members of a group use their cars for the outing, the others are helpers. The hosts have a group to tea in their home once or twice a year.

There are now some 4,000 people involved with Contact groups. For each one of them their commitment to Contact's particular way of trying to help lonely old people involves their time and their energy. Each driver in a

111

Contact group provides his/her car for the outing. Each host provides her home and tea.

We do not recruit volunteers specifically to shop, to garden, to visit regularly or to do those things which are difficult when you are no longer supple and confident. Yet all these things can happen within a Contact group when people get to know each other; when relationships are established. Greater involvement occurs, spontaneously paced by the volunteer and the elderly person.

We define the framework. The people in the groups take up the idea and make it their own. In this way it is their responsibility, and therefore their sense of satisfaction and fulfilment is more direct.

We believe that this kind of partnership between statutory and voluntary services will be a formula for caring for the ever-increasing numbers of elderly people who will be with us into their 80s. Not just because the demand for services is always likely to exceed the supply, but because we believe that people need to give and to feel valued. A Contact group provides a channel for these energies for people of all ages, while at the same time giving vital and much-needed support to the lonely and vulnerable older members of society.

*Contact address:*
CONTACT
15 Henrietta Street
Covent Garden
London WC2E 8QH.

# VI
# Conclusion and Speculations

The projects we have described do not amount to a new type of social service. But they do represent a distinct social ideal: an effort to develop patterns of social care that put special emphasis on *informality, reciprocity and locality*. Although this ideal is not unique to members of Good Neighbour Schemes, we do feel that the evidence we have gathered demonstrates that, among such schemes, the ideal is being pursued with particular dedication and wholeheartedness. In the last analysis, *that* is what makes Good Neighbour Schemes an important venture in social policy and an important object of study.

Furthermore, it seems that, under certain conditions and within certain limits, their efforts can achieve significant success. The absolutely crucial problem seems to be that of matching care to need – and of doing so in ways that permit the growth of friendly, mutually supportive relationships among all the local residents concerned. Of the many aspects of this problem suggested by our survey, we wish to stress seven particularly obvious points: (i) *the need for dialogue* between neighbourhood projects and the statutory and voluntary services around them; (ii) *the need for practical advice and information* to enhance the confidence and competence of actual and prospective members of Good Neighbour Schemes; (iii) *the need for cash* and, more generally, for a sustained input of resources over and above what the members of schemes can contribute on their own; (iv) *the need for community links*, between schemes and a host of other local ventures and activities; (v) *the need for a closer understanding of the points of view of the recipients of care*, to break down the barriers of mistrust that so often exist between the members of schemes and local residents in general; (vi) *the need for a clear sense of priorities* in the range of activities and objectives that Good Neighbour Schemes pursue; and, related to that, (vii) *the need to accept and support a measure of formal organisation* as the unavoidable means of promoting informal neighbourly relationships. In turn, each of these needs presents a double challenge: a challenge to local residents to act more effectively for themselves, and a challenge to our established social services to make room for neighbourhood care.

## The Need for Dialogue
The fate of Good Neighbour Schemes in a given area is, to a large extent, in

113

the hands of the social services authorities and major voluntary organisations already operating there. If schemes are to flourish, these authorities must accept the ideals of "grass-roots" neighbourhood care as a matter of positive policy. And the members and organisers of schemes must learn to live with a measure of outside interference and with constant demands for accountability that may seem quite at odds with their basic ideal of informal neighbourly care. Each side must work out a way of co-existing and co-operating with the other which recognises that, beyond their common interest in providing care, they function on very different principles. Working towards a dialogue in which information, referrals, advice and support flow readily in both directions is a delicate task. It calls for considerable negotiation, experiment and compromise on both sides, if schemes are to become effective agents of social care without at the same time losing the distinctive local identity and energy that is the key to their ability to cultivate neighbourliness. And it requires both sides to recognise limits to their own field of action. There is much that Good Neighbour Schemes cannot do, and there is much that statutory authorities need not do. In each neighbourhood, a precise division of labour adapted to the needs of that neighbourhood has to be worked out.

## The Need for Advice

We have repeatedly seen how willingness to help in principle can be inhibited in practice by a fear of not knowing just what to do or how to do it. Lack of confidence, a sense that one is simply not competent, is a major reason for the shortage of helpers experienced by so many schemes. By contrast, confidence in one's personal competence, often based on long practical experience, seems to be a hallmark of many of those who play the most active part in organising and supporting successful schemes. Competence can, however, be acquired. And it can be acquired either through direct experience or through indirect "educational" means. Perhaps what is needed is a much more wide-ranging and carefully-considered campaign, through both direct and indirect channels, to increase the competence of actual and prospective Good Neighbours. So far as direct action is concerned, the relative success of those schemes that do make a deliberate effort to bolster the confidence of their helpers by a careful matching of people to tasks can hardly be ignored. In indirect terms, much more could be done in the way of information, advice, even training, and, above all, in the *pooling of relevant experience* both locally, through meetings, discussions and newsletters, and nationally, perhaps through a more concerted and comprehensive information exchange.

## The Need for Cash

We have seen that, at present, organised Good Neighbouring is dependent upon relative personal prosperity. The costs of being a Good Neighbour can be high, and the rewards often modest. Part of this problem is no doubt psychological; but a good deal of it is downright material – witness the chronic difficulty schemes have in providing transport. Despite the assurance of so many Good Neighbours that "money wouldn't make any difference; I'd do it anyway", and despite the need to protect the spirit of volunteering implicit in such remarks, it is obvious that, in many instances, money and other forms of material support would make a difference, often a decisive difference to the success of the scheme. To bring the real costs of effective Good Neighbouring into the open and to demand that they be met is therefore essential. It is simply unrealistic to expect "doing good" to be its own reward when, in so many respects, it is tiring, anxiety-provoking and expensive. More realistic is the conclusion reached by so many of our informants that their schemes would have been successful had they had a paid organiser or some other form of regular resource. Most people who join Good Neighbour Schemes do so on the basis of what Diana Leat has called "limited liability". They have many other commitments that they are unwilling or unable to sacrifice, however keen their enthusiasm for Good Neighbouring. At the same time, the range of needs for care that schemes may be asked to meet, and the tasks of co-ordination, communication, advice and support involved in meeting those needs, are complex and demanding. Many schemes survive because of the extraordinary devotion and energy of one or a few "central figures". But the supply of such people is strictly limited – and, even among them, few can endure the burden of sustaining an effective scheme for very long. For a neighbourhood of, say, 5,000 households, the work involved is equivalent to that of a full-time job. And back-up resources of cash are also needed to produce newsletters, provide transport, meet the incidental expenses of helpers, or pay the rent of that indispensable telephone or office. How can one hope to secure reliability of commitment if being seriously out of pocket can be a hazard of giving care in a world that is hazardous enough already?

## The Need for Community Links

Many schemes seem to exist in a curious state of isolation within their own communities; the Hope Green project is a good example. Here our conclusions must be rather more speculative, but it appears that schemes can reap much benefit from involvement with a wide variety of other local groups, activities and ventures. Among our case studies, the Good Neighbour Schemes in both Reaching and Greenwich gained energy and support because their attempt to organise neighbourhood care was closely bound up with other community projects and with a more general *advocacy* of local interests. Nor can one help noticing that these wider community links are often of an essentially *political* nature. The Greenwich project was connected with a Tenants' Association and also with a wider campaign for pensioners' rights. The Reaching Good Neighbours were closely associated with the efforts of a Community Association to protect various local amenities. So perhaps it is not simply wider community links that matter, but the kind of links that involve a scheme in some visible *struggle* on behalf of the neighbourhood. Perhaps the important point is to link neighbourhood care to neighbourhood action, to be prepared to adopt a combative as well as a caring posture. Evidence from the United States – where 'neighborhoodism' in general is much more established – seems to support this suggestion. Instead of developing into a form of "service delivery" – the local aspect of a welfare system in which the "strong" care for the "weak" – Good Neighbouring should perhaps be seen as an assertion of the ability of ordinary citizens to act independently of that system.

## The Need to Understand the Point of View of Recipients

Any attempt to base neighbourhood care on the genuine interests and attitudes of local residents would demand a much clearer knowledge of, and deeper respect for, the point of view of the recipients of care than most schemes seem to possess at present. This knowledge is, in part, a practical necessity; it is the way to break down the barrier of mistrust that separates people in need of care from people willing to give it. But it is also important for the *principle* of neighbourhood care. Such care depends for its effectiveness on the positive involvement of *all* concerned; to that end, such conventional social work notions as "clients" and "referrals" (let alone "cases") should be eliminated from the vocabulary of Good Neighbour Schemes. Genuine Good Neighbouring depends on a recognition of the common interests of "helpers" and "helped" simply as people and as residents of a shared neighbourhood. To detach Good Neighbouring from traditional images of "charity", one must therefore start by finding out a great deal more about the wishes and feelings of those to whom help is offered – not least, what they themselves can offer their "helpers". Above all, this knowledge should be treated with respect. Failing that, Good Neighbouring is likely to degenerate into just another, rather inefficient, branch of "the welfare".

## The Need for Priorities

Generally speaking, Good Neighbour Schemes are involved in three distinct types of activity. They "monitor" need within their neighbourhood, keeping an eye on local residents and passing on information about those who may need help. They also themselves provide various kinds of help and practical care. And, most distinctively, they engage in a wide range of activities intended to promote general "neighbourliness". Our conclusion is that, of these tasks, monitoring is the one that Good Neighbour Schemes do best, and the one that allows them to be most readily seen as fitting into established patterns of social care. But, against this, we must also point out than many schemes have convincingly demonstrated that the local organisation of care can promote neighbourliness, and that the simple practical tasks involved can be the vital medium through which caring services are transformed into neighbourly personal relationships. The danger is that these practical tasks will assume undue importance in their own right; that Good Neighbours will come to see themselves as mainly, or even exclusively, people who visit, shop, drive, or collect prescriptions, and that the ultimate aim of cultivating neighbourliness will be pushed into the background. When what happens, it is difficult for schemes to counter the criticism that they are in various ways less effective or less reliable than the alternative service-providers, the statutory and major voluntary organisations. If Good Neighbour Schemes are to avoid being judged as simply amateur and unreliable versions of already-existing social services, they may need to insist more emphatically that the promotion of neighbourliness is their top priority, to which the monitoring of need and the carrying-out of practical caring tasks are subsidiary.

## The Need for Formal Organisation

All Good Neighbour Schemes embody a paradox. They exist to promote informal social relationships, above all those of neighbourly care. But they do so, and can only do so, on the basis of competent formal organisation. Their problem is to develop a type of formal organisation that will permit aims to be clarified, helpers to be mobilised and tasks to be assigned, yet will not compromise the basic informality that makes such schemes a distinctive and important feature of our welfare system. It is, for many schemes, a matter of establishing an informal pattern of day-to-day activity within the shell of a formal system of responsibilities, structures and relationships. Again, the balance is easier to describe in theory than to achieve in practice. The Pitside scheme is one example of how it *can* be achieved – but an example that depended on the fact that strong networks of informal neighbourly relations existed in the community before the Good Neighbour Scheme came into existence. We could cite many examples where, lacking that favourable context, schemes have quite failed to implant themselves in their neighbourhoods. And there are just as many instances of schemes deeply attached to informality that have failed to develop as either monitoring or care-giving networks for want of the essential hard-headed, impersonal element of formal organisation. We see no way in which this paradox can be avoided. The challenge is to find patterns of organisation that permit the pursuit of neighbourliness – formal frameworks for the cultivation of informality.

In principle, this challenge could probably be met. Schemes throughout the country are attempting many different ways of tackling it and, although we have not discovered any single scheme that we can hold up as having solved all the problems, we hope that this book has shown that many have

117

taken important steps towards solving one, some or even many of them. In other words, somewhere within the collective experience of Good Neighbour Schemes as a whole there may be a recipe for dealing with the fundamental issues that face them all. If our conclusions about what is needed are less than complete, we hope that out readers will fill out the picture by drawing their own.